CENTERING

Navigating Race, Authenticity,
and Power in Ministry

CENTERING

Navigating Race, Authenticity, and Power in Ministry

MITRA RAHNEMA, EDITOR

Committee for Antiracism, Anti-Oppression,
and Multiculturalism of the Unitarian Universalist
Ministers Association

Skinner House Books
BOSTON

Copyright © 2017 by the Unitarian Universalist Ministers Association.
All rights reserved. Published by Skinner House Books, an imprint of the
Unitarian Universalist Association, a liberal religious organization with more
than 1,000 congregations in the U.S. and Canada, 24 Farnsworth St., Boston,
MA 02210–1409.

www.skinnerhouse.org

Printed in the United States

Cover design by Kathryn Sky-Peck
Text design by Jeff Miller

print ISBN: 978-1-55896-799-1
eBook ISBN: 978-1-55896-800-4

6 5 4 3 2 1
19 18 17

Library of Congress Cataloging-in-Publication Data

Names: Rahnema, Mitra, editor.
Title: Centering : navigating race, authenticity, and power in ministry /
    Mitra Rahnema, editor, Committee for Antiracism, Anti-oppression, and
    Multiculturalism of the Unitarian Universalist Ministers Association.
Description: Boston : Skinner House Books, 2017. | Description based on print
    version record and CIP data provided by publisher; resource not viewed.
Identifiers: LCCN 2017008670 (print) | LCCN 2017020849 (ebook) |
    ISBN 9781558968004 | ISBN 9781558967991 (pbk. : alk. paper)
Subjects: LCSH: Unitarian Universalist churches. | Race relations—Religious
    Aspects—Unitarian Universalist churches. | Pastoral theology—Unitarian
    Universalist churches. | Interpersonal relations—Religious Aspects—
    Unitarian Universalist churches.
Classification: LCC BX9841.3 (ebook) | LCC BX9841.3 .C46 2017 (print) |
    DDC 262/.14913208996073—dc23
LC record available at https://lccn.loc.gov/2017008670

This book is dedicated to the
Reverend Doctor Orlanda Brugnola
1946 – 2016

Thank you for authentically and powerfully dedicating
yourself toward a multicultural and honest Unitarian
Universalism that could make room for all.

As we move through life
finding ourselves

always wise and newly foolish,

we ask that our mistakes be small
and not hurtful.

We ask that as we gain experience

we do not forget our innocence,
for they are both part of the whole.

—Rev. Dr. Orlanda Brugnola

Acknowledgments

We would like to give a special thank you to the following:

Thank you to all the writers in this book. We thank you for sharing your experience, wisdom, and heart with the world. Together we are stronger.

Thank you to Josh Pawelek for his "yes" to this book idea. Your "yes" and work to design the project made everything possible. Also, thank you for all the ways you dedicate yourself, with integrity, toward creating spaces for people of color and addressing oppression throughout Unitarian Universalism.

Thank you to Don Southworth, UUMA Executive Director, for his incredible support over the years. Without your expertise and leadership we would not know where to begin.

Thank you to Mary Benard, Editorial Director of Skinner House Books. From the beginning, and consistently throughout the project, your enthusiasm, support, and thoughtful antioppressive work made this project possible.

Thank you to the Unitarian Universalist Funding Program for granting the money needed to allow for the conversation to exist.

Thank you to Janice Marie Johnson of the Unitarian Universalist Multicultural Ministries Team in the Multicultural Growth and Witness staff group of the UUA for your support in launching the project.

This book was imagined, created, and led by two iterations of the Ministers' Association Committee on Anti-racism, Anti-oppression, and Multiculturalism. They are:

2013–2016
Josh Pawelek
Nori Rost
Lauren Smith
Walter LeFlore
Mitra Rahnema

2016–
Walter LeFlore
Wendy Williams
Josh Pawelek
Summer Albayati
Robin Tanner
Duncan Teague
Mitra Rahnema

We all have family and friends who were a special part of the creation of this book in a variety of ways. We offer a collective thank you for your support, time, and care throughout the years.

Language Note

As a general rule, we have capitalized *Black* and *White* because they are cultural as well as racial identifiers and used the gender-inclusive term *Latinx* instead of *Latino*. We have also lowercased the term *people of color* according to standard practice and because it is an umbrella term rather than a specific identity. However, we have deferred to contributors' personal preferences regarding this terminology upon request.

CONTENTS

Introduction

Words like *marginalized* and *decentering* are often used to talk about identity, systemic oppression, and authenticity. These are limited words, as all words are, yet they are part of what we currently have to describe both experiences and systems that are oppressive. The oppression can be overt, but more commonly, it is implicitly embedded in a culture that is assumed or considered normative, and therefore unrecognized. We all have parts of our individual lives that are marginalized, such as emotions, longings, and hopes. We are complicit in that marginalization of our own selves and the pressures of what is deemed acceptable in society. Our Unitarian Universalist faith calls each of us to center that which has been marginalized within. It is what we do.

People of color are marginalized based on a racial identity by the system of society. We call this *institutional marginalization*. Over time, people of color have found power and meaning in being on the margins. We gather under the marginalized umbrella. When we come together in community, we grow stronger, we are reminded that we are not alone, and we experience both solace and hope. Ultimately when we are in community with those on the margins, we are putting our voices and experiences at the center, discerning our own truth and what we want to do with it, grounding ourselves in love, and remembering our most authentic selves. Together, we are centering that which has been marginalized.

Often the religious professional is one of the most visible and invisible people in the communities with which we offer our ministry. We are highly visible in the pulpit, coordinating a program, speaking at a rally, teaching, providing pastoral support, offering counsel, or even given special attention at a meeting. Very few are aware of the work and attention given to listening, observing, researching, planning, supporting, discerning, and writing. It is commonly said that 80 percent of what a minister does is unrecognized yet vital to the success of a ministry.

Similarly, often a person of color is one of the most visible and invisible people in a culturally White faith community. A person may be highly visible by the way they look, or by name, language, accent or tone, or simply because of the energy created by a felt difference in culture. Yet, a person of color's personhood, unique beauty, struggles, spirit, identity, and experiences are invisible to the White community, often because of assumptions, projections, bias, micro-aggression, and discrimination. It is common to hear in culturally White communities some version of "When I look at you I don't see race. I just see human." Yet people of color do not have the option to experience life this way, which means our experiences become invisible. The visibilizing of people of color and the subsequent invisibilizing work together to create perceptions that we just don't fit.

For religious professionals of color, a whirlwind of simultaneous visible and invisible experiences is generated by the layering of our chosen profession on top of a historically marginalized racial identity. It becomes a unique position filled with stories about navigating these experiences. These stories are profoundly valuable for our understanding of a community's culture and building support for one another.

You may have heard the riddle about a father and son who are in a horrible car crash. The dad dies and the son is rushed to the hospital. As he is about to go into surgery, the surgeon stops and says, "I can't operate. This is my son!" We are asked, "How is that possible?" The riddle intends to point out gender assumptions. It muddles us because we forget the possibility that the surgeon could be a woman. Furthermore, even posers of this riddle tend to forget an alternative answer, that the son could have two dads.

Similarly, Unitarian Universalism, like much of the larger culture it inhabits, is burdened with the assumption that a minister is White, in addition usually to able-bodied, heterosexual, married, and cis male. Each category of religious professional comes with its own assumptions. These assumptions manifest themselves throughout the preparation for any kind of ministry, continuing education, collegial conversations, congregational life, and interfaith collaboration. Basically, we encounter them everywhere we turn. Therefore, most conversations and trainings about things like diversity/multiculturalism, right relationship, and anti-oppression put White experience at the center—learning to reach out and be relevant to people of color. Rarely are the leadership and experience of people of color at the center of the conversation. In short, people of color spend a lot of time learning about the White experience of people of color. In these conversations and trainings, the presumption that the intended audience is White moves religious professionals of color to the margins of the conversation and doesn't help us become better ministers. Meanwhile, we want to share our experiences, learn, and grow in ways that are relevant and transformative too. We want to explore the ways we negotiate the racial divides, identity, authenticity, and power and how to keep centering ourselves in the hearts, minds, and words of our faith.

The Unitarian Universalist Ministers Association's Committee on Anti-racism, Anti-oppression, and Multiculturalism (CARAOM) was especially motivated to undertake a project that centered the needs and experiences of people of color. This book attempts to do just that, to center the stories, analysis, and insight of people of color who are offering religious leadership.

We believe that topics like how people of color can exercise power effectively, be relevant, and connect to others in culturally White settings belong at the center of Unitarian Universalism's anti-oppressive work. Religious professionals of color are here and have been here working in liberal, culturally White faith communities for a long time. Therefore it seems to CARAOM not only appropriate but essential to place our struggles, experiences, and reflections at the center of our collective learning. It is imperative that we explore how racial identity is made visible and invisible by our profession.

When we began this book project we thought centering that which is marginalized would be a new paradigm for anti-oppression educating and organizing. We focused on lifting up the voices of religious professionals of color, which also had the effect of asking people of color to center ourselves in our own consciousness. Ironically, we found that when people of color get together we demonstrate our own tendency to center Whiteness, we talk about what White culture is doing. During the course of this project, we all were amazed at how difficult it was to set a White-centered narrative aside to center our own narrative.

We focused on religious leaders because the work of joining the journeys of congregations, larger communities, colleagues, and the denomination requires us to constantly contend with the tensions between visibility and invisibility as people of color. We honor that there are many who have similar experiences of marginalization and many of our contributors hold multiple identities that are all part of the constellation of self, yet we focused on people of color in order to further a new vision of anti-oppression work. We recognize that is just one piece of the puzzle of oppression. *Religious professional* is a broad term that incorporates many people offering ministry, including music directors, membership professionals, religious educators, and ordained clergy.

Ministry is something we all do. The nine chapters and responses included in this book are almost all written by ordained clergy, with one non-ordained professional religious educator. In no way does this book fully represent all religious professionals. It doesn't even include all the ordained clergy perspectives that should be told. We wish for more professional and racial diversity as part of collegial solidarity for people of color. We hope this is a starting point toward centering the stories of religious professionals of color and their relationship with their own ministry.

We wanted to create a body of work offered primarily to an audience of religious professionals of color from their colleagues of color. We asked contributors to share not only their stories and reflections but the tools they have used to navigate their ministries. We always held the intention that we are not trying to teach the collective Unitarian Universalism; we are simply lifting up and honoring the complex stories and useful skills of some of our leaders to be shared with one another and with those yet to come. Personally, I wish I had this resource from the beginning of my ministry, but as Susan Newman Moore said in our conference, "If what you need and want is not there, create it."

The project began with an open invitation for essayists. We sought a mix of congregational and community ministries as well as seasoned and newer leaders. We also looked for a mix of ages, sexual orientation, and racial identities. Then we looked for essays that would touch on some specific ministerial roles—Prophet, Pastor, Preacher, Community Organizer, Educator, Administrator, Scholar. Once the initial essays were selected, we paired each essayist with a respondent.

In October of 2015, CARAOM members, most essayists, and respondents came together for a reading and discussion of each essay and response. It was a moving weekend during which we took the time to listen, recognize, and learn from one another. We talked not just about the organizing umbrella of "people of color" but about the unique relationship we each have with our own identity and ministry. We contended with questions of authority, humility, differentiation, and being exposed. It was a rich sharing. Much of our dialogue was recorded. The quotes sprinkled throughout the text are from those conversations.

After our conference, during our editing phases, we lost one of our writers, Orlanda Brugnola, who died very suddenly in February of 2016. She was one of our respondents but hadn't had the opportunity to prepare her response for publication. Our hearts ache for the loss of a powerful and loving religious leader. We are also grateful that Leslie Takahashi agreed to offer her wise response to Hope Johnson's essay in Orlanda's stead.

Throughout the project, several themes emerged. The themes are tensions that all religious professionals navigate, but when layered with a racial identity they become prominent and particularly nuanced. They are all interwoven with issues of role authority and of racial marginalization. These themes are explored in a section called Discussion Cues at the end of this book, and I hope people of color will use these to catalyze conversation within your Unitarian Universalist communities. May these cues offer strength, inspiration, and guidance as you navigate the terrain of your leadership.

This book contains the powerful and tender stories of real people at the forefront of Unitarian Universalism's growing edge—people whose experiences with Unitarian Universalism and beyond are shaping the direction of our faith. Each essay and each response is a treasure. To be sure, they don't all agree with each other, but if we want our faith to survive and thrive in a future that looks more and more precarious with each passing day, these are the voices we must listen to. I ask that you refrain from reading this book too fast; take in the texts as living, breathing testimonies of faith. The stories are embodied, so believe them and allow them to touch your heart and soul. We made the commitment to stand by the integrity and vulnerability of our writers, and we ask that all our readers engage their witness with loving hearts.

The completion of this project comes at a unique time in history. We were putting the finishing touches on our manuscript as United States President Barack Obama's eight years came to an end. He certainly represents the apex of leadership as a person of color within a culturally White system. We watched him navigate identity and leadership in both prophetic and pastoral ways. As I write this introduction, the shock waves of new priorities are hitting us and the future of our country's engagement with issues of race and identity is much more uncertain. The values of respect, dignity, learning from one another, and solidarity despite our imperfections and disagreements require us to rise up and say, "We believe." We hope this book will stir new imaginings about how to do that.

May this be a new beginning, a new paradigm for creating sustainable, multiculturally competent communities of faith. May we build strength for and among all religious professionals of color and all people who know in their bones what it means to live on the margins and be centered.

—Rev. Mitra Rahnema
April, 2017

OTHERING AND BELONGING
Rev. Darrick Jackson

In the wake of Ferguson and the Black Lives Matter movement, I have found my Unitarian Universalist identity and my African-American identity at odds. These recent events have brought to light, once again, my struggle with being in a faith that is sympathetic to my identity as a person of color but just does not get it.

Not long after, in the wake of the shooting of Michael Brown in Ferguson, Missouri, I attended a vigil hosted by one of our UU congregations. We stood outside holding candles and sang songs of justice. We went back inside, and all the ministers processed. We listened to prayers and reflections from ministers in the community, UU and otherwise. As I looked out at the sea of mostly White faces, I felt alone and isolated instead of drawn into the community. It was clear to me that my UU community was looking at this issue from a distance. They were supporting justice for the "other." In that moment they saw me only as a Unitarian Universalist. They saw the police violence as something that happened to "other people"; Michael Brown did not represent their brother, son, nephew, cousin. They were outraged about the injustice; I was feeling the pain of my people. I saw no space to name that pain in my UU community, at least not with people who would understand. I did not need a sympathetic ear; I needed someone who could understand my pain and could help me find solace in our UU faith. But that was work I had to do on my own, and it required resources outside our UU faith and grounded in African-American tradition.

We always talk about meeting people where they are.
How about meeting them where we are? When is there
ministry to ask people to meet me where I am at as a
person of color? To ask you to see me for what I am
and meet me there?

REV. ADAM ROBERSMITH

And so I wonder: If I cannot find the resources for spiritual development within our faith, how am I expected to effectively minister as a person of color?

I was a Universalist before I even knew there was a religious home for my beliefs. And yet, I still go back to the spirit of the African Methodist Episcopal Church within which I was raised. I often ache for the music that makes my heart soar, that brings the divine into the room during worship. I miss ministry that is grounded in and speaks to my Black identity. I miss a message of hope that is grounded in an understanding of struggle. I miss all these things, and yet theologically I can be nowhere else than where I am. So I make my home here in Unitarian Universalism, as imperfect as it is, and find ways to stay grounded, to stay connected, and to stay whole.

Growing up in the AME Church, I was presented with images of spirituality grounded in my black identity. The worship service and religious education both referenced Black history and Black culture. I learned how my cultural struggle and my identity interfaced with the biblical narrative. When I became a Unitarian Universalist, it was clear that my history and my culture were not reflected in the worship and religious education. I could connect on the level of my humanity, but my identity was rarely represented except on special days: Martin Luther King Jr. Day, Black

History Month, and Kwanzaa. In those moments, I felt *other*. I felt that my culture was being put on display, not an inclusive part of the service.

As a minister, I have been invited several times to do a Kwanzaa service, and each time I have declined. My own observation of Kwanzaa has waned over the years, and it did not feel authentic to lead a group of mostly White congregants in a celebration of Black culture and identity. When Kwanzaa was an important part of my spiritual celebration, and before I was ordained, I did share Kwanzaa with my church as a part of a celebration of winter holidays. That felt comfortable to me, as it was part of a larger celebration, and Kwanzaa was important to me and something I could share. However, I was troubled the first time a member of the congregation asked me to help them observe Kwanzaa. This request did not feel like an invitation to share but an attempt to co-opt something that had meaning for me without an understanding of the context from which it came. They even went so far as to ask me to procure the ritual elements for them. I was offended that they would want to appropriate my holiday and wanted my assistance to do it. I told them that I was not comfortable with helping, and with some explaining, they understood why I wouldn't.

———

Unitarian Universalism's longing for diversity makes us,
as people of color, points of access in bringing that
longing alive. In essence, we have to deal with a certain
level of imposed marginalization—irrespective of how we
see ourselves. Unitarian Universalism sees us and needs
us at the margins as a way of relating to the other that is
often missing from or underrepresented in our pews.

REV. MANISH MISHRA-MARZETTI

I also see UUs make assumptions about what would interest me as a Black person, without ever asking me. I have preached at several congregations where the music director has chosen spirituals for the music because I was the preacher. The spirituals were often sung without any awareness of what the music means or how to sing it. It requires a lot of energy to sit in front of the congregation and not let your real feelings about the music show on your face, or to figure out how to respond to the eager faces of the choir looking for approval.

As a worship leader, I have had difficulty finding UU resources for my services, particularly when dealing with issues of struggle, despair, grace, and hope. Our hymnal deals with struggle through justice and despair through loss. It briefly engages hope and barely refers to grace at all. Growing up in the Black church, these themes were an essential part of my understanding of worship. The service created space to name the truth that life was sometimes hard, unfair, and painful. We sang songs filled with tears as well as joy, and we were offered messages of hope. My Black church responded to the unfairness present in our everyday lives and gave us a reason to keep on striving to make things better. When I engage with other Unitarian Universalists, these are themes they want to explore, regardless of their racial identity.

The AME Church has also informed how I think about music for worship. I like to begin the service with reflective music and end with music that is energetic and engaging. But our hymnal does not support that idea. Most of the hymns are medium to slow and tepid in their musical arrangement. I am rarely able to find music that fits the energy I am trying to engender. Often I work with the musician to play hymns and not dirges. And even if the musician gets it, the congregation slows it back down.

Music can evoke a deep spiritual strength in me that helps me transcend the issues and concerns in my life. In worship, it can help me connect with the theme for the service in a visceral way.

But most UU hymns feel like vehicles for the words, n experience of the holy. Until *Singing the Journey* was p few hymns popular among UUs could be vehicles for t_ _..._ scendent, and most of the ones that did came out of the African-American tradition.

This is indicative of the mental focus of UU worship. Words are primary; we think and talk about spirituality but are hesitant to experience it. In the Black church I experienced worship that engages body, mind, heart, and soul. But I see many UUs hesitant to engage the heart, the body, and the soul. They only want to stimulate the mind. They look for sermons that make them think and find sermons that stir the heart lacking. I have had to make peace within myself about my preaching, as I have no interest in the intellectual sermon. I want to touch the heart, to nurture the soul. My sermons are intellectually informed but rarely intellectually focused. In fact, my least favorite sermons are my intellectual ones.

The intellectualism in Unitarian Universalism comes with a culture of stillness. We are expected to sit quietly in our seats, listen intently with no emotion on our faces, no movement in our bodies. We are supposed to wait until after the service to express ourselves. I grew up in a culture of engagement. We had permission to respond to the service, to say Amen when we were moved by the words or music, to clap our hands and smile and nod our heads whenever the spirit moved us. We lived the hymn "When the Spirit Says Do" every time we gathered for worship. I have had to learn to restrain myself in UU circles, which distances me from the worship. Sometimes our worship feels more like a lecture to me. The first time I preached at a UU congregation, I was unsure of how my sermon was being received because there was no visible response. It wasn't until after the service that I learned that people did enjoy the sermon. Even now, I get slightly unnerved by the lack of response. I construct my services with UU

*I like to think of power as a positive force. It's helpful
to me to look at the kinds of power that I can step into
at any given moment, how I can attend to my own
needs in a system that may be damaging. Is there any
place to name the ways we are messed up by the things
congregants sometimes do, in addition to taking it up
with them one-on-one? Is there any way to name
that in the congregation with integrity?*

REV. LAUREN SMITH

———

stillness in mind; any attempt at a more embodied worship feels experimental and risky instead of one of many ways worship happens. I have always loved youth and young adult worship, as those services are generally more heart- and soul-centered and invite engagement and connection.

Engaging UUs in conversation about these areas where I feel disconnected from the UU culture is hard. I often struggle with how to say something, or if it is worth it. I worry about the other person's reaction, and I have to decide if I have the energy to deal with it. Often when I engage with someone about these matters, the conversation quickly turns to them (how they feel about it, how they are not to blame, and so on); instead of engaging the issue, I'm engaging their needs. I minister to them pastorally instead of prophetically. Tied into this is my own struggle with wanting to engage in multicultural ministry because it is important, not just because I am a person of color. Because of this, I prefer to engage people I know well, who I know will not respond defensively. I struggle with this because the line between avoiding conflict and self-care feels very narrow in these situations.

My connection with UU people of color has been essential. Through DRUUMM (Diverse Revolutionary Unitarian Universalist Ministries), the Finding Our Way Home retreats, and individual friends and colleagues, I have found this community to be a stabilizing force in my life and ministry. Being able to share experiences and not having to explain why they are important or troubling helps normalize what is happening for me. Sometimes I receive great advice, and sometimes I just need to be heard and acknowledged, and that is enough. Either way, I leave these encounters renewed, restored, and ready to reenter the broader UU life.

Gospel music still elicits joy within me and gives me a sense of peace and a reminder of hope. I find myself singing along and smiling, rapt in the power of spirit and the hope that things will get better, just as I did when I was Christian. Gospel music is the place where I can reconnect with my Christian roots in ways that are healing and life engendering, even though I no longer connect to the theology. I have written new words to my favorite songs and have thought about writing UU gospel music. Unitarian Universalism has a gospel message to share, and listening to the music reminds me of the saving power of our faith.

The Harlem Renaissance, one of my academic and artistic interests, is another source I am drawn to when I need words of grounding, of comfort, and of joy. I have researched and explored

---

I know the sadness of trying to find the good news for the congregation in our tradition, which I embrace, but which also troubles my spirit. There is an urgency for me in finding joy in this faith, and that core of sadness is a barrier.

REV. DR. WILLIAM SINKFORD

the writings of this period and used them in worship, in centerings, and as the basis of a one-person show. They speak to me and provide me additional resources within which to engage the themes of despair, grace, and hope, as well as other themes, which I have difficulty finding in Unitarian Universalism.

Spiritual practice has been essential for my grounding in Unitarian Universalism, and in ministry. I have been drawn to Pagan ritual and practices, which provide for me that connection to spirit that is embodied, heartfelt, and soulful. Walking meditations, labyrinths, and knitting all help me connect to the spiritual through movement. These balance the heady focus of traditional UU worship and provide me what I am missing on Sunday morning.

We as people of color broaden the experience of Unitarian Universalism. What is it that we bring? What is it about our experience that broadens and deepens what Unitarian Universalism is or ought to be?

REV. WALTER LEFLORE

As a minister, I search for ways to create for others what I have found missing in Unitarian Universalism. I incorporate the voices of people of color in worship throughout the year, not just for special occasions or topics. As much as I can, I engage the body and the heart as well as the mind. I am conscious of creating spaces for connection and engagement in worship, instead of stillness and isolation. I try to be attentive to the experiences of my seminarians of color as they find their ministerial path.

As a community minister, I intentionally sought a worship community that addressed as many of my concerns about the broader UU culture as possible. Having a minister who is also a person of color has been extremely helpful in sustaining me, so that I can be effectively ministered to as I minister to others. We all have to find our resources and supports so that we can minister effectively as people of color. At this point, our needs as people of color are broader than what the faith can fulfill, but I hope that we can live into our stated dreams and be a faith that is open to diversity in both word and deed, and that I am able to bring my full self, my full spiritual, worshipping self, into our faith.

RESPONSE TO DARRICK JACKSON
Rev. Lilia Cuervo

EVER SINCE I CAME to the United States from Colombia, I have tried to understand the dissonance between my ideas about myself and my ideas about this, my adopted country, and what my experience has been. I learned through the years that everyone born and living south of the Rio Grande is considered a person of color and therefore inferior. I learned that Americans believe the myth of their manifest destiny and that we are part of the "White man's burden." I learned that whenever the economy is booming, the need for cheap and slave labor increases and Latinxs are enticed to come to work here. Yet when the economic tide turns, they are made scapegoats for the ills of the economy. I learned that until recently, except for migrant workers, the Latinx population has been the "invisible" minority.

Similarly, since becoming a Unitarian Universalist, I have tried to understand the dissonance between what I expected my new religion would add to my spiritual life and what experience has taught me. That is why I empathize with Darrick's observation that the UU culture "is sympathetic to my identity as a person of color but just does not get it." The gap between *sympathy* and *getting it* may be due in part to the fact that, since its birth in America and still to this day, UU culture has perfectly reflected the nation's culture. And that is precisely what makes it difficult to bridge the gap. The following seem to me to be important points of convergence and fusion between the two cultures:

- A sense of exceptionalism, deeply rooted in ignorance, results in disregard of and disdain for other nations and cultures. Americans and UUs continue to live the myth that we generally enjoy a superior socioeconomic status, with greater class, wealth, and education than others. This prevents us from acting justly toward the many among us who don't fit that myth. It also prevents us from meeting and inviting the "other" to our exclusive clan. We view missionary churches with contempt and find no need to share our UU gospel.
- A culture of dominance and entitlement is reflected in top-down influence. We impose our own brand of democracy and extract what we want from other cultures. We UUs practice top-down social justice by doing *for* others when we should work *with* others, inviting them to our religious home and participating in worship and social justice work in their midst.
- The demographic configuration—Like our country, our denomination is one of immigrants, albeit from other traditions. The invitation "Give me your theologically abused, the traditionally oppressed, the spiritually homeless" aptly describes our intention to be the liberal religion that not only welcomes but also gladly includes all who are drawn to us. Both our country and our denomination have the potential

------

There was an instance during a workshop when I expressed my feelings of sadness about having been bullied by someone in the congregation. A person of color took me aside and scolded me for my disclosure. She said that, as her minister, I was supposed to be strong and not drag her down with me in front of the White people.

REV. LILIA CUERVO

to be made greater by a rich mix of all kinds of peoples, cultures, and religions. Unfortunately, as in the country, our welcome and acceptance are preferential toward those "like us." Our collective experience has taught us that to succeed in this denomination, persons of color, and I would say ministers of color in particular, need to display strong survival abilities to endure microaggression, bullying, and disrespectful challenges to our authority. It does not take much to realize that our Unitarian Universalist elitism, both cultural and theological, born and rooted in the halls of Harvard, has been detrimental to our growth and to our democratic aspiration to be one faith open to, compassionate toward, and accepting of all.

• Both Americans and Unitarian Universalists can take freedom of expression to its extreme. We UUs claim to detest dogma; yet we are capable of acting and speaking in a self-righteous and chastising manner: "In this church we don't wear *that* (usually a cross) or say the G word or like Pagan rituals." This is especially hurtful to seekers of color who come to us searching for a liberal faith but who still treasure, at least at the beginning, some of the symbols and rituals of their native faiths. An employee of color of the congregation I was serving confided in me his bewilderment and humiliation when a congregant, without asking permission, hid under the shirt of the employee the cross he was wearing.

• U.S. anti-federalism fractures the unity of the country and makes it difficult to offer an even distribution of goods and services throughout the country. UU congregational polity also makes it extremely unlikely that the Unitarian Universalist Association can adopt a core belief and that our ministers would choose to preach a similar gospel of hope and redemption in all our congregations. This variously affects those seekers, including people of color, coming from faiths with dogma or unified beliefs. Although rejecting dogma, it took me a

> *I live this "inherent worth and dignity." I come*
> *to it honestly. I am UU, so this is what Unitarian*
> *Universalism is. We speak a language of immigrants,*
> *but White UUs don't claim themselves as immigrants*
> *because they reject our native tongue.*

REV. WALTER LEFLORE

———

while to feel safe theologically since I was led to believe that I
could believe almost anything I wanted and change my beliefs
whenever they didn't feel right.

- A confusing manifestation of UU polity is the variety of names
  adopted by our congregations to indicate their theology or
  lack of it: Society, Church, Parish, Congregation, Fellowship.
  I witnessed the hurtful treatment accorded a newcomer by
  an indignant old timer who scolded him for using the word
  church since this word "offended the humanists and the Jews
  among us."

- UU congregational polity has resulted in a disjointed emphasis on the spiritual and the pastoral mission among our congregations. Individuals seeking spiritual depth are lucky if their
  local church offers that which they seek. Although dissatisfied
  with what they experience in Sunday worship, many people
  keep attending because the UU congregation is the only liberal
  religious place in town. Darrick expresses a similar sentiment
  when he writes, "I miss all these things, and yet theologically
  I can be nowhere else." Both the confusing variety of names
  adopted by our congregations and the disparity in theological
  orientation offered by them make it very difficult for all kinds
  of seekers, including people of color, to readily match that
  which they seek with what is available to them.

- The American concept of self-reliance, intended to inspire and encourage the insecure and the timid, can lead to blame and despair. In our religious body, self-reliance can deter the soul from seeking union with and strength from the Mystery and can make one shy away from the benefits of praise and petitionary prayer. Many a UU minister has found his or her theology of self-reliance lacking in compassion when most needed—such as at the bedside of the dying and in the presence of the depressed. Darrick's lament seems to confirm the sense of isolation our UU faith can bring: "They were outraged about the injustice; I was feeling the pain of my people. . . . But that was work I had to do on my own, and it required resources outside our UU faith and grounded in African-American tradition." I have been surprised and disturbed to learn of the number of colleagues and ministers going to counselors and spiritual directors from other religious persuasions. I have been asked, "Who are we to pretend to spiritually guide or direct anybody, particularly other UUs?" Ex-Catholics, especially from Latina America, accustomed to confession and to frequent one-to-one spiritual guidance may feel spiritually underserved in our fellowships and less spiritual congregations. Fortunately, now we have a growing list of ministerial and lay UU spiritual directors.
- The Americans have short attention spans and are attracted to the new and the exotic, the breaking news. Similarly, UU congregations like what is trendy and start all sorts of social justice projects, many of them short lived and uncompleted, as their success depends on the enthusiasm and persistence of a few sponsors. It is not a secret that several well-intended projects to attract people of color were eliminated or allowed to die when the novelty wore out, when they became too culturally challenging, or when the money required to sustain

them dried up. The latter cause is often a consequence of the pervading culture of scarcity.

- In the United States, the richest country in the world, a prevailing culture of scarcity is reflected in tight budgets for projects that would benefit those most in need of assistance. This culture pervades the great majority of UU congregations as well. Even those with million-dollar endowments and assets devote unusual amounts of time to discussing budgets that reflect this fear of scarcity and limit the reach they could have. Despite stated good intentions of becoming multiethnic and multicultural, there are few examples of successful congregations in this regard. Coupled with a general lack of interest in attracting people of color, there is always the excuse of tight budgets and decreasing pledges.

- The gap between sympathy and "getting it" is magnified by the fact that the Unitarian Universalist faith has tried to be open to all, pleasing to all. In the process, its spiritual and theological roots have been replaced, for the most part, by secular and rational thought, to the point that the church lacks a clear understanding of its secular goals and its religious vision and mission. Somehow we ended up substituting emphasis on social justice, which benefits mostly Whites, for emphasis on what should be the truly inclusive, multicultural, antiracist prophetic and visionary voice and deeds of the church. Unless religious leaders decide to extricate this faith from its pervading secularism, UUs will continue paying lip service to our wish for spiritual growth and transformation. UU ministers are called to use our prophetic and pastoral voices from the pulpit and take every opportunity to preach the Unitarian Universalist gospel. However, unless we get serious about living and preaching that gospel, we will be unable to provide true religious homes that would cater to the spiritual and emotional needs of the thousands of seekers—many of them people of color. Unless we courageously use our prophetic, compassionate, and healing voices to attract and keep newcomers well nurtured spiritually and emotionally, our congregations will continue being proverbial revolving doors.

Darrick says, "For me, worship is an experience that engages body, mind, heart, and soul. But I see many UUs hesitant to engage the heart, the body, and the soul." It is the same with me. Once I liberate my mind, my body feels free to move, to clap, to feel alive during worship. My heart aches seeing so many people in our pews restraining their desire to give in to joy through movement, frozen by fear of judgment. That is why, in my first sermon at First Parish in Cambridge, I promised that sooner or later I would have them dancing. I fulfilled my promise, and it was a happy day for me when, during a Day of the Dead service, five couples spontaneously, one by one, proceeded to dance in the aisles to the mariachi music.

Just by being present, a minister of color not only changes the makeup of a congregation but, if allowed to exercise leadership, helps over time to create an environment in which transformation can happen in small and big ways. I have been fortunate to have made many contributions to the life of the congregations I have served, such as inaugurating and leading Day of the Dead (Dia de los Muertos), a Blessing of the Animals, bereavement support groups, an End of Life Fair, and annual bereavement support groups. Some of these contributions relate directly to my identity as a minister of color, and others were possible because I was allowed to use my authority and to exercise my leadership.

As a Latina, I have modeled a spirit of welcome and hospitality and have called congregations to pay attention to inclusiveness across culture and class, and continue to do so. For example, I educated them on the importance of food in offering authentic welcome. I have also encouraged congregations to incorporate Spanish in worship, music, signage, and other public communication. One of the most rewarding outcomes of my efforts has been the increased use in worship of *Las voces del camino*, the Spanish-language hymnal, which I helped to initiate and contributed to.

I found a big difference between the Catholic services of my youth and UU services, particularly in the preaching. Unlike the priests, who delivered their sermons *ad libitum*, UU ministers preach from a written text, and their sermons often resemble a lecture. Having been encouraged to preach this way, I now regret having suppressed for so long my passion and spontaneity in the pulpit, to the point that I doubt I can ever fully regain it.

Little by little, I internalized detachment from my Judeo-Christian roots and from the culture of honoring my spiritual ancestors, a detachment modeled persistently by many ordained and lay church leaders. After a major epiphany regarding that loss, I have been discovering anew the riches and comfort of those roots and that culture.

My rapid acculturation in this country was facilitated by the fact that, in my country of origin, I was given a mostly Euro-centric, humanistic education. But since becoming a UU, I have gone through three main cultural paradigm shifts. The first began one Sunday after I had been a Unitarian Universalist for some fourteen years. A member of my congregation approached me saying, "The Unitarian Universalist Association wants to know how many people of color there are in the denomination. Could you please fill out this questionnaire?" I couldn't figure out why he asked me. Driving home, I was stunned to realize that after all these years of feeling at home in UU congregations, I was considered a person of color with all its hurtful implications. Discovering that how others perceived me was different from how I saw myself was very disconcerting. That was the first shift. The second shift happened when I pre-candidated at a certain congregation. After I was told that I was one of two finalists and a great match, a member of the Search Committee asked me, "How are we going to tell the congregation that we chose you, when they are expecting a person of color?" After much wrestling with the idea of accepting my new diminished status, I finally had been feeling comfortable as a person of color, only to be told, at this important juncture in my life, that I was not one. Having worked for so many years for multiculturalism and against prejudice and racism, I decided to go back to my true identity, so firmly imbued in me by my

---

I keep coming back to the question of which truths do we tell. What responsibility do we have to tell all the truth all the time or none of the truth none of the time, some of the truth some of the time? How do I make those choices, and how do I feel good about those choices? When do they have integrity? When are they motivated by fear? When are they motivated by ministry? When are they motivated by the real self as opposed to the self that other people see me as in my light-skinned, blond-haired, blue-eyedness? I'm thinking about what's at the center and who's at the center. What I have come to is that I am at the center when I have the agency to choose my own actions. I may not always choose well or wisely. I might get it wrong, but when I feel like I'm centered, when I have the ability to make a choice, not have it forced on me by the outside, not feeling like I have to comply with somebody else's perspective on who or what I should be, then I see myself healthfully at the center of those choices.

REV. ADAM ROBERSMITH

mother. I am a child of the universe, my people are humanity, and I owe my accountability to the indwelling Mystery in me. I continue, and will until I die, to follow my call to be a bridge between traditional dividers: cultures, generations, ethnicities, religions, and age. Thus, I have circled back and arrived at my third and, I hope, last paradigm shift.

Darrick tells us, "At this point, our needs as people of color are broader than what our faith can fulfill." I also struggled for years, especially when I was doing full-time parish ministry, to find within UU communities spiritually nurturing and enriching opportunities for my soul. I am grateful that I now have two churches where, in the company of others, I enjoy prayer, meditation, and inspirational worship. I am also blessed to be a member of a special group of nurturing and inspirational UU colleagues, the UU Mystic Ministers small group I founded, and the UU Women Ministers Meditation group, both under the auspices of the Massachusetts Bay Area UUMA.

———

I just have this thing in me that says, "If what you need and want is not there, create it. Step out of the box. I get tired of dealing with what White folks' assumptions are and how I need to transform the power. But sometimes it's like that hymn says, "New occasions teach new duties. Time makes ancient truths uncouth." There comes a time that you've got to do something new. When there are new people coming, someone has to walk with them. And I'm saying that I think we are coming into a time, and maybe are in a time, that we need to catch that vision. I don't know what it is, but it's something stirring.

REV. DR. SUSAN NEWMAN MOORE

Hiding from the Beloved, Hiding from Authenticity

Rev. Summer Albayati

M Y PATH TO ORDAINED MINISTRY began long before I knew that was my destination. I was in college in 1991 when the United States invaded Iraq. Stories of Saddam Hussein terrorizing Iraqis flooded the Arab-American community as the proponents of the invasion sought justification. I heard threats that we Arab Muslim Americans would be put into internment camps, just like Japanese Americans during World War II. My family worried about how we would survive and wondered which neighbors would take us in. I watched and listened as members of the community came together to share their own stories of pain and as Arab Muslims disappeared from our communities. I realized that we were no longer considered Americans. We were truly the other, and *otherness* was institutionalized.

Although I felt tension between wanting to hide my identity and wanting to fight for justice, something pulled me into a new way of life, a life of continually speaking out against oppression. This divine experience, known as God in Islam, has a way of reminding you to be your authentic self. As I spoke out, I became known as an Arab and a Muslim. Of course, with authenticity and standing up for oppressed peoples came more hatred and racism than I had ever experienced before—including from a tenured professor in a field in which I had hoped to pursue a PhD. After college, speaking out for justice threatened both my livelihood and my friendships.

I want to lift up the profound psychospiritual cost of passing. It is not just guilt but also the loss of family, the loss of culture, and the loss of connection, the loss of spirituality and faith and grounding. It forces generations that follow to fight to re-center themselves, especially in the context of White fragility. We actually expect passing on multiple levels from our religious professionals, particularly religious professionals of color. How are we dehumanizing our religious leaders through our own expectation of passing?

REV. SOFIA BETANCOURT

———

These experiences taught me how to "cope" with racism. I *learned* to keep my mouth shut. I *learned* to put up with racist remarks. I *learned* to use joking as a coping mechanism. I *learned* to act even more White—dressing in socially acceptable clothing, styling my hair in socially acceptable ways, joining groups that were socially acceptable, and never publically showing my feelings about the oppressions I and many others experienced.

The thing about God is that you cannot get away with hiding for too long. This divine energy kept calling me to be my authentic self. Though light-skinned and thus able to pass for White, I no longer passed once I revealed who I was and what I stood for. As long as I spoke out against injustice against Arabs and Muslims, I was viewed differently and no longer belonged in the club.

As my country fought a "war on terror," I realized that if I was to be a part of this oppressed community, I would also need to be a part of liberating the oppressor by teaching those from the dominant culture about their own inherent racism. Unbeknownst to me, these feelings served as a first calling to a life of ministry, to serve by working toward justice.

In seminary, I found myself in a multicultural setting in which some professors actually encouraged me to write and study about the experiences of Arab-American Muslims. I could share my own experiences of racism openly in some classes. In other classes I dared not to reveal myself as Arab or Muslim; even my identity as a Unitarian Universalist was only mildly accepted. After all, I was still at a Christian seminary. But those professors who welcomed my lived experience began to heal some of the pain of my experience.

Seminary became a sanctuary of love as I searched within for the voice of the *Muslimah* (Arabic for "female Muslim"). But there were exceptions. When I received this love and preached about Islam in a sermon that focused on the similarities among various faiths—including Christianity, Judaism, and Buddhism—

"This reminds some Unitarian Universalists of . . ."
is used often as a justification for silencing almost
anything in our communities. This is the fear that we
will create some tiny place of discomfort, some memory
of early pain, some small sense of lack of inclusion, and
that is used to justify massive lack of inclusion. We are
severely limited by that phrase. How can we as religious
leaders start to undermine the notion that it is okay for
a personal small moment of discomfort to silence an
entire tradition, an entire people, an entire faith
perspective in our congregations?

REV. SOFIA BETANCOURT

I was told that my speaking of Islam reminded some Unitarian Universalist congregants of terrorism. Of course, this had the effect of silencing my voice yet again. The message I heard was that I could never preach about Islam.

I experience this tension as an Arab-American Muslim Unitarian Universalist minister. I feel I can speak about my Sufi ancestors but not my Muslim family.

I've had so many conversations with UU ministers from the Middle East who said they won't preach about the Middle East, and I have definitely found in congregations, especially those that have many folks of Jewish descent, that this is the one issue that will not be touched, where we won't stand up for Palestinians in the world. We'll stand up for Syrian refugees—it's safe to talk about them. It's safe to even talk about the Iraqi refugees. It's not safe to talk about what's happening with the Palestinians.

AISHA HAUSER

There is another unspoken tension here: I cannot fight for justice in the same way non-Arab and non-Muslim Unitarian Universalist ministers do. I am Arab and Muslim, and that, unfortunately, trumps any privilege or protection afforded me as an ordained Unitarian Universalist minister. Instead, I must tread softly as I educate our denomination in the beauty of Islam, the fears that Muslim Americans face when they enter our own sanctuaries.

Since social justice brought me to Unitarian Universalism, I wonder how to deal with the daily messages that we ministers of color are not quite up to par if we do not participate in the risky behaviors some of our White colleagues and congregants can and do participate in. How can I live out the promise we Unitarian Universalist ministers preach about, that we will dedicate ourselves to justice, without risking arrest or my family's safety? How do I live with the shame I feel when members of the congregation I serve risk getting arrested for a social justice cause that they believe in, while I have visions of Guantanamo, internment camps, and White supremacist police if I participate alongside these members? How do I explain to them that these visions haunt me and prohibit me from participating in such a noble experience with them? How do I express my deep sorrow at choosing to work for justice in a less radical way, when all I want to do is feel free enough to have that choice to behave in such a radical act of love?

The pain is real. When my congregants ask why I'm not at a protest, I pray they'll remember that I am not just a minister but a human being as well. When I am targeted and searched at yet another airport because I carry the proud name of my Iraqi ancestors, tears form in my eyes because I know that once again my minister identity and light skin have not protected me.

See, I have been spat upon by a White supremacist when I was in the vicinity of a protest against the invasion of my beloved Iraq. Though I was on my way to my car and could have been just another person walking down Hollywood Boulevard, the hatred emanating from the eyes of this man and the assault on my face reminded me that I can try to hide, but hatred and oppression will find me.

The Beloved will bring me back home. But what of this concept of the Beloved?

Many of us sing the well-known verses "Come, come whoever you are, / wanderer, worshipper, lover of leaving. / Ours is no caravan of despair. / Come, yet again, come." These lines probably inform a theology that was taught to me by my father. A concept of forgiveness and love is infused in these lines. God, or the Beloved, will love you even though you are not perfect and make mistakes and leave yet again. The Beloved awaits you with hope, not despair. Of the ninety-nine names for the Beloved, the ones most often on the lips of Muslims are *Rahman*, or Merciful (forgiving), and *Rahim*, or Compassionate (loving).

And so it is with these concepts on my heart that I must ask how we, a beloved association of congregations, show compassion and truly love the other—forgiving ourselves, being merciful toward ourselves as God is merciful with us when we fall short.

My late Iraqi Muslim father taught me this concept of forgiveness by saying, "An eye for an eye and a tooth for a tooth, but if you forgive, God will forgive." This concept of forgiveness was big in our home. I learned that God will forgive me when I forgive others. This is an aspect of the Beloved that I have taken into my ministry. I have to remember that through the growing pains of working through centuries of learned hatred toward Arabs and Muslims, our beloved communities and association must be forgiven. If I forgive, God will forgive me. If I forgive you, I can forgive myself.

Since 2001, when we all watched a vicious terrorist act upon American soil, the interest in Islam has increased. If one were to ask any Muslim on the street, they would probably agree that this was not the act of Muslims but terrorists. Yet Arab Americans, in particular Arab-American Muslim women, have become the focus of search and rescue missions as we "liberate" them from oppressive husbands and fathers. There is a race to become the hero and rescue the Arab-American Muslim woman from herself. But as a minister of color and a woman, and certainly as an Arab-American Muslim woman, I have never had a need to be rescued. The only rescuing I needed was from my own feelings of anger and hatred toward those who were taught that White is better than "other." They are also victims of a racist system. My only rescuer was the Beloved. When I experience yet another racist comment within our congregations, what sustains me is my belief that working for justice is working for God. *Sabr wa iman* is Arabic for "patience and faith." This Islamic concept enables me to work steadfastly toward our beloved community.

Hate crimes toward Arabs and Muslims have increased since 9/11 and again in the wake of the 2016 election. Racist images have paraded across American television and movie screens for decades. In the face of this, I ask myself every day what I, as a minister and a woman of faith, can do to help this beautiful liberal faith of mine let go of the thousands of years of programming about Arab Muslims.

I am an Iraqi-American minister living in a culture that vilifies the other. Both cultures are part of me; I am part of two countries that have been at war for most of my life. So I have to wrestle with how to help our congregations learn that their beliefs may not be their own, that they have been manipulated by fear to support a war against their beloved minister's family. Yes, my family. They have fled their homeland, the site of the Garden of Eden and Noah's ark, the birthplace of Abraham. They once lived in a country known as the "cradle of civilization," in which the first writing and literature, mathematics, astronomy, and laws were formed. This minister's family lives as refugees. Every Iraqi American, every Arab American, every Muslim immigrant who has seen the effects of war lives between this liminal state of hopelessness and hope as we witness hearts change within and beyond the Americas at the same time that wars on terrorism continue. *Sabr wa iman.* Patience and faith. Keep the faith.

I believe the Beloved wants us to see the other in each other's eyes—a mirror reflection of the soul. Jalal'a'din Rumi tells a story regarding this concept. A contest is put forth between the Chinese and Greeks, each claiming they are better than the other. The Sultan brings the Chinese a palette of colors, at their request. The Greeks request polish and cloths. Separated by a curtain each goes to work. When they finish, the Sultan returns and opens the curtain. The Chinese artwork is the most beautiful he has seen, especially its reflection on the polished walls. He says that the Greeks are like the Sufis who polish away, purifying their hearts from greed, lust, envy, and hatred (Masnavi 1:3467–84).

Can Unitarian Universalism ever purify its collective heart from hatred toward Arabs and Muslims?

I stand here boldly declaring that I am the face we have learned to fear. And I am a Unitarian Universalist minister. I am present and strong and a spiritual leader. I am here to help our denomination cast aside fear of the other. I must write about Islam, preach about Islam, speak about the concepts that make Islam an amazing religion with more than a billion followers worldwide. I must educate people about why this religion is beautiful and why Arabs and Muslims are not to be feared. I was called to this Unitarian Universalist faith for a reason. It is because I believe Islam calls on Muslims to embrace all religions and is closer to Unitarian Universalism than other religions may be. Islam calls on us to strive toward justice, as Unitarian Universalism does.

And so I boldly speak out, but I recognize that this is quite a task for one minister of Arab and Muslim descent. Writing this essay as a response to the need to polish our hearts is one way that I help liberate our denomination and liberate myself for the Beloved and for my own authentic self.

As I write about others and share my own lived experience, I follow the bold teachings of our Unitarian Universalist ancestors such as Thomas Starr King, who called on people of faith to stand with the other and end slavery and terrorism. I stand with the ancestral voice of Martin Luther King Jr., who called on

I told the social justice folks in my congregation when I first came that when they say to me, "We need you here. We need your voice. We need your presence," I will bend heaven and earth to be there when they need me in those spots. But there is one thing I will not do and that's get arrested. As a queer person, as a person of Romany (Gypsy) descent, I come from people who hide in the woods from the police. We do not put ourselves in their way. I can't stand seeing a cop in a car on the street. My heart pounds out of my chest. I told them right up front, "Don't expect this from me because it's not happening unless it's by accident." Even talking about it, I can feel myself getting tense and scared. There's some privilege around getting arrested and not actually getting in trouble. It's kind of a public naughtiness that's okay. There are people for whom that is powerful and it has made a difference in the world, and I don't want to denigrate that, but I do think it's important to recognize that there are more facets to that conversation than a lot of our movement allows for, and that sometimes we feel like we don't have a choice. The question is, do I have the choice to say yes or to say no, and I don't always think that I do.

REV. ADAM ROBERSMITH

people of faith to join in Selma—to fight the occupation of terror. This is not easy. It is a test of inner strength to speak when silenced. Our ministerial presence brings a story of hope, and it is lived out loud in the pages of a book.

And I call on others within our denomination to be courageous and speak of the liminal states we traverse as spiritual leaders and persons of color, learning to serve and change culture within our Unitarian Universalist beloved communities so that the other truly feels welcome in our sanctuaries. We also must ask ourselves how we might be cultivating the culture of fear when we hide from the real stories of Arabs and Muslims sitting within our congregations, thus furthering a cultural stereotype. For the Muslim adult or child looking to be held in the loving embrace of God, how will we provide a sanctuary of healing rather than another place of terror? How will we confront our unintended racism in order to genuinely welcome them? As a minister, I am not perfect. I fail every day. But I must look within when I live out the stereotypes taught to me by a culture that has an interest in perpetuating stereotypes. I play a part in continuing the stereotype when I do not do the work of transforming my soul to one of love and acceptance and forgiveness. And so I wonder, how can our congregations become sanctuaries of freedom and hope? How can we free the chains that bind us and keep us from truly living our Principles?

We have an opportunity here to change the outcome of the story. Perhaps by committing to learning about Islam, studying the Qur'an, and building partnerships with those who identify as culturally Muslim, we can unravel the cultural stereotypes and fears that are embedded in our own American identity and begin to transform our beliefs so that when a young unmosqued Muslim family enters our sanctuaries in search of true sanctuary and love, we don't inadvertently say something that alienates and "others" them.

I am committed to creating a multicultural denomination, and this is why I continue to serve even when words hurt me. I forgive because I know that congregants and colleagues do not realize what they are saying or doing. They, like I, are products of a culture that has demonized the other—usually the brown- or black-skinned other; the other with exotic eyes and accents and thick, curly hair; the other who eats different foods and listens to different music, the other who has different family experiences, the other who has experienced institutionalized racism and must cope every day in order to feed their families. I must begin with forgiving myself and asking for forgiveness as I continue to free myself from the chains that keep me oppressed and the images that keep me acting as the oppressor as well.

And yet I witness in our beautiful congregations, the beloveds standing together holding hands, sometimes swaying to the music, affirming that they will stand on the side of love while embracing the person with an accent sitting next to them. I am filled with hope and love, because this denomination creates heaven every time we fill the sanctuary with love—if only for an hour or a moment. Learning to truly love is how we will be saved. When

---

It's clear that, for Summer, God and Islam are foundational and feed and strengthen her. Where do we as Unitarian Universalists find the courage to speak our truth? Is there something within Unitarian Universalism that feeds that, that supports that, that gives us that strength? I don't know that it's truly there. It feels like there's something sorely missing. But is it always our job as people of color to transform our faith?

REV. WALTER LEFLORE

we create the beloved community every day, we will become salvation for others.

Unitarian Universalism can bring more persons of color, including Arabs and other Muslim Americans, into our love fest, not because we wish to "liberate" them in an imperialist way but because we have something beautiful to offer them in a culture that vilifies them.

If there is a denomination that can succeed in creating a multicultural denomination, it is Unitarian Universalism. I believe our congregations will learn to embrace the other in such a profound way that we will end up liberating ourselves over and over again.

RESPONSE TO SUMMER ALBAYATI
Rev. Dr. William Sinkford

R ESPONDING TO Summer's writing is a privilege. Several elements of her story have similarities with my story. Similar experience helps foster connection. But some elements of her story are quite different from my experience. There is richness in those differences but also challenge.

It plays out differently for me, particularly as an African-American male minister, because images of African-American male ministers are pretty well established in the culture for White folks. They have a pretty clear idea about who we are supposed to be.

REV. DR. WILLIAM SINKFORD

Do we approach one another analytically and in judgment? Or is our approach openhearted and appreciative?

At times in Unitarian Universalism's engagement with issues of race and diversity, judgment about our differences has prevented appreciation; it has been more important to some of us to be right than to be kind. In these matters, which touch our identities and our calling so directly, a culture of care and a covenant of respect seem essential.

One gift I bring to this process is personal history with our faith's attempts to engage with diversities of race, ethnicity, and

I've been in gatherings of ministers of color where people
got skewered, and it has been super painful.

REV. LAUREN SMITH

———————

culture. Over thirty years of service to UU congregations and the
Unitarian Universalist Association, I have seen substantial change
in our ministry. Twenty-five years ago, fewer than two handfuls
of African-American ministers, seminarians, and potential seminarians came together for support in the African-American Unitarian Universalist Ministry.

Today, the number of ministers of color in our faith approaches
one hundred, the Unitarian Universalists Ministers Association's
responsibility to support ministers of color has been named and
in place for more than fifteen years, ministers of color now serve
three of our largest congregations, and the last two UUA presi-
dents have been ministers of color.

But the progress has not been even and certainly not effort-
less. Change in our congregational cultures remains very much
a work in process. Ministers of color in congregational settings
are often cast as change agents, if not racial and cultural saviors.

———————

The last time the Association went around the issues of
race and culture seriously, it became so divisive and was
handled so badly by people digging in their heels and,
frankly, taking idolatrous positions of righteousness,
innocence, and justice and casting a pall of wrongness,
sin, and injustice on everybody who disagreed with
them. We need to do it better this time.

REV. DR. WILLIAM SINKFORD

———

Within my life of being a UU, which is approaching twenty years, there's been a really nice, lovely shift in tone within our communities of color. The past year is the first year I've stepped back into these types of discussions because they frustrated me so much. One thing I've been really struck by is that we are holding one another in a way that feels so much more loving, humane, and compassionate. We are seeing and holding one another in authenticity more than we ever have before. I'm sure there's still work we could do, but I've been really touched by the progress. In earlier years, there were times when our conversations felt like: "I'm sharing the Asian experience, and you're not going to get it because your experience or perspective is something else." At times the discussions even felt like they were at cross-purposes or framed as zero-sum games. But now it seems we can gather without feeling we have to establish that some group's hardship is more difficult than another group's hardship. Where we are today, as a community of color, is just beautiful and feels really good.

REV. MANISH MISHRA-MARZETTI

———

My history doesn't necessarily connect me to the struggles of other people who have also struggled. I have committed the sin of believing that no people have struggled like my people. And Unitarian Universalism is where I've learned any solidarity with other people. It's in Unitarian Universalism that my love for people has been expanded beyond my love for Black people, because I do love me some Black people, but Unitarian Universalism has asked me to enlarge my heart, to keep growing, and that's what I need. It's for me to personally expand my circle of concern and live that out.

REV. NATALIE MAXWELL FENIMORE

––––––––

Addressing the complexities of ministry that we face in such a role is an important conversation for the UU Ministers Association to host.

One important shift that has taken place during this time is welcoming ministers of color with a variety of ethnic and cultural identities. Asian, Indian, Filipino, Native American, Hispanic, and Arab UU ministers serve our faith. And religious diversity has expanded as well. Hindu UUs and Muslim UUs now join the traditional Jewish and Buddhist UUs who are part of almost every UU congregation.

We have always been a hyphenating people, comfortable with multisyllabic names, more so now than ever. The term *minister of color* embraces a much wider range of identity and lived experience than was the case twenty-five years ago. The cultural contexts span a greater range as well. But the African-American experience still dominates the narrative within the liberal community, though how long that will be the case is an open question. The Latinx community, in number, is larger. It is more bicultural and bilingual, the oppression less evident—perhaps.

As an African American, I know that the well-educated, liberal White congregants to whom I minister share a basic orientation to me and the racial identity I represent. This orientation dances around a guilt, or at least sense of responsibility, about slavery and the oppression of African Americans in this country. Even if they reject personal guilt or responsibility, these congregants have a knowing that oppression was visited on "my people" by "their people," and that knowing operates in the background and grants me some strange and unearned kind of moral authority. The reaction of liberal White UUs to Latinx ministers, Native American ministers, and Japanese and Chinese American ministers carries some of the same charge of responsibility for mistreatment by the White majority in this country.

The liberal White reaction to an Arab and Muslim UU minister, I believe, may function without that charge of guilt or even sense of responsibility. Because guilt is so much a part of the

————

There is this one-degree-of-separation comfort that happens so that I can say my ancestors were oppressive to your ancestors, and therefore I should listen to your authority. We've actually come a long way and lived into that. We don't do well when the oppression of now is on the table. This is now. The war on terrorism is today. What I hear is "I don't want to talk about how my people are oppressing your family now. I want to talk about how my ancestors did. Let me heal that wound rather than acknowledge the active wounding I am doing today."

REV. SOFIA BETANCOURT

reaction I have received, I am not at all sure what the dynamics of ministry would look like without the moral authority it has granted me. On what source of moral authority could an Arab Muslim UU minister rely? Could White congregants justify a claim of innocence and resist appeals to responsibility? Would it be easier or more difficult for them to stretch to understand and know their minister? Because American culture has made terrorists of all Muslims, and Arabs generally, the White culture can wear the mantle of innocence with greater comfort than they can in relation to other racial or cultural identity groups that "we" (the United States) have oppressed.

Perhaps I resonated most with Summer's story when it highlighted the concerns she must hold that never need trouble our White colleagues. Her concerns (being seen as a terrorist) are somewhat different from mine. But I know that my White congregants do not share the anxiety I feel when approached by a White police officer—and never will. The experience of living with dual realities in Summer's story feels very familiar. And though she does not name it, I wonder if the danger of forgetting that we are seen as the other is not part of her struggle. Does she get surprised sometimes when she realizes she is being seen as an Arab Muslim woman minister, when she thought she was serving as just a minister?

Passing is no longer is a possibility for Summer. I hear that as central to her call: "The thing about God is that you cannot get away with hiding for too long. This divine energy kept calling me to be my authentic self." Being out about who we are means different things and brings different dangers for ministers of color. That is something Summer and I share: "Though light skinned and thus able to pass for White, I no longer passed once I revealed who I was and what I stood for."

But here again, differences are present. In my family, passing as White was the goal. My birth certificate says I am White. That was seen as protection for me, I am sure, by my parents, who themselves were passing for White in California when I was born.

Being out, embracing my identity, has had many benefits for me: affirmative action in college, early corporate job placements, seminary scholarships, and perhaps my rapid rise to denominational leadership. That affirmative action does not apply for Arab and Muslim UU ministers. Embracing my heritage closed off few options,. For Summer, embracing her heritage and identity clearly cuts off the comfort that would have been hers by identifying with the White majority culture, by passing.

The experience of passing carries with it a guilt born of betrayal of who we are and a constant fear of being outed. A ministry of authenticity seems so difficult when conducted from the closet. The Beloved, to use Summer's language, would call constantly for honesty, troubling the spirit.

Late in her essay, Summer issues her call: "I call on others within our denomination to be courageous and speak of the liminal states we traverse as spiritual leaders and persons of color, learning to serve and change culture within our Unitarian Universalist beloved communities so that the other truly feels welcome."

"To serve and change culture." Does service to our congregations as they exist today cast ministers of color only in the role of change agents? Is it failure if we serve without the constant demand for change? Are we comforting the comfortable rather than afflicting them? How much change can we demand and still survive as pastors?

These are $64,000 questions for ministers of color. Is my success in parish ministry to be measured in the same way as it is for my White colleagues, by congregational growth or fund-raising performance? Or does my success depend on change in congregational demographics, more dark faces and greater credibility in the broader communities of color? Why is it my job to change

Being in a Unitarian Universalist congregation as its minister means that, for many people, no matter what I am inside, I'm passing. I'm passing as middle class. I'm passing as overeducated. I'm passing as one of them and giving them comfort that someone of color can be in their midst in a way that makes them comfortable. So I stand in the Labor Day service and say, "My folks made cars in Detroit, I know what hard work is. This is who I am." I stand up after Ferguson and say, "I lived in the city in the middle of a riot. My home was searched by the National Guard. At nine years old I saw the biggest guns I have ever seen, and so I am not comforted by security people in the airport." I do feel that we have a disproportionate calling to push back against the ways that people are putting us in a box and asking us to pass for what we are not, and to be clear about the variety of experiences we have. So I do have to stand and say, "I'm not speaking for all Black people, for all people of color, but this is my experience, and you need to recognize that we have a variety of experiences that we hope you will welcome into this place."

REV. NATALIE MAXWELL FENIMORE

When I was thinking about whether to submit for this book, I asked some colleagues who are not of color, and the responses I got were basically not to do it. So in the face of that, I asked myself, "Should I do this? I'm fairly new in this ministry career. What could it do? I could never get a position. I could lose my current position." But I also said to myself, "We have to be our authentic selves. We have to speak our truth, because if we don't, we only have ourselves to blame." I said yes because otherwise I wouldn't be true to my own people, to my family.

REV. SUMMER ALBAYATI

Sometimes I say "no" to the expectations of diversity and being a person of color. I'm going to find my authentic self and, in doing so, try to redefine what the expectations are. That has probably limited my ministry. But I think I am just trying to find some way in which to put myself at the center in order to navigate what that means for ministry.

REV. MITRA RAHNEMA

UU culture? More and more White colleagues own that transformative work. Yet that task seems never to leave my to-do list.

I have been trying to find a way to change the complexion of Unitarian Universalism virtually all my life. If I knew how to do that, to be the leaven in the UU loaf, we would all be living in the promised land, all thriving on multicultural breads: flatbread, pita, nan, cornbread, as well as whole-grain and gluten-free recipes.

I still feel called to work for that transformation in our faith. In my own ministry in Portland, we constantly do "trainings" (beloved conversations, gatherings with White allies). I am blessed to have White colleagues who help our most committed folks understand how to be allies and supporters of efforts led by people of color to oppose the new Jim Crow. And we hang the Black Lives Matter banner prominently on the front of the church. I know the complexity of preaching from my identity. How often can I preach on race? How often can gospel be our musical vocabulary? And can Malcolm X be a theological resource for us alongside Martin Luther King Jr.?

But I must plead guilty to the dynamic Summer identifies with regard to Islam. We love Rumi and can tolerate Hafiz. The mystical tradition of Sufism is comfortable for me and for us. I am only now investing a modest amount of energy in learning more about Islam.

In fact, I wonder whether the prominence of the African-American experience might make the Arab and Muslim experience with its different history more difficult to communicate, or even more difficult for White UUs to value. To what extent has the African-American narrative of oppression become part of the normative culture that presses down on Summer, making it harder for her to be seen as all she is?

The ministry of identity has been one of our faith's strengths. Our witness and work on LGBTQ issues and marriage equality has helped define us for a couple of decades. But identities are complex and multifaceted creations. In the hierarchy of privilege and oppression, most of us experience some of both. In the politics of power and oppression in the United States, I have always been a second-class citizen, even when I was benefitting from affirmative action. I've never had a safe haven to lose.

I remember so well realizing that in one day, September 11, 2001, African Americans ceased to be seen as the most dangerous

I am not Arab or Muslim, and yet as an Iranian American, I faced the ramifications of the war on terror my entire life. I have been called, and know what it means to have people wonder if I am, a terrorist. It is awful. Now, as leader of a congregation visibly partnering the local Black Lives Matter group, I don't want the label terrorist *to be applied to them by association. I want to protect them from it. I don't know what to do about that because I also don't want to center our partnership conversation on my identity experience. It's complicated.*

REV. MITRA RAHNEMA

---

people in America. But I greeted that change with only sadness and no relief. Adding one more group that must struggle for acceptance and empowerment is not a cause for celebration.

And I remember, every day, that the beloved community will be incomplete until we can sing, "Come, come, whoever you are," and mean at least all those who are called to our ministry.

CALL AND RESPONSE
Rev. Lauren Smith

WE'RE ALL PART of an unfolding personal and communal human story whose ending has not yet been determined. My job as a preacher is to plumb the wisdom of our religious tradition, including its Sources, to help guide those stories in the direction of wholeness, peace, liberation, and life. The sermon brings the wisdom of our source traditions to bear on the challenges of human existence, which may relate to the personal lives of individuals, to a particular community, or to humanity as a whole. Each of us participates in life at all these levels.

My emerging voice is also shaped significantly by my particular call to ministry.

We need to highlight the wealth of experience, the wealth of knowledge, the wealth of education, the wealth of culture—all these things that we bring. Some of them are invisible or barely visible, and the congregations and the world need to know what we are here to do, that we can do it a very excellent way, and that we are even more talented than many senior ministers who have been squashing us. Ministers of color bring the love. We bring the warmth, the compassion. So this kind of contribution cannot be just ignored. We need to put it out there.

REV. LILIA CUERVO

I am called to serve at the intersection of Unitarian Universalism and black communities. This call to ministry became clear to me after a lengthy period of discernment and exploration and is the warm coal at the center of my ministry, the living center from which so much else emerges. My relationship to my sense of call became complicated in the fall of 2010 when I went into search for a senior ministry position, along with my husband, Chris. We had our sights set on only one congregation, the Unitarian Universalist Church of Portsmouth, New Hampshire (known as South Church).

I found myself in a bit of a pickle as I entered my information into the online service for UU congregations seeking a minister and UU ministers seeking a congregation. At first, I pasted in language I had crafted for the Ministerial Fellowship Committee so that I could tweak it. It began with "I am called to serve at the intersection of Unitarian Universalism and black communities." But this was the bind: I found it hard to imagine that sentence about serving at the intersection of Unitarian Universalism and black communities would seem relevant to a search committee in Portsmouth, New Hampshire. I was concerned it would raise immediate red flags. I was applying for a ministry position in a predominantly white church in one of the whitest states in the nation.

So I deleted the sentence.

But of course I couldn't just delete my call to ministry. The symbolism of striking out that particular sentence in order to get a job broke my heart.

So I put it back.

In the end, all went well. My husband and I were ultimately called to Portsmouth, and it's a wonderful fit. We have every hope of spending the next twenty years here, as we imagined. But the conflict that expressed itself as I typed in (and deleted and typed in again) my ministerial record has remained a core tension of my ministry. That tension expresses itself in a number of ways when it comes to my ongoing development as a worship leader.

Portsmouth has been a great surprise in a number of ways. It is the least racially diverse community I have ever lived in, which is sometimes hard. But it has a small and active black community. As one of just a few black ministers on the New Hampshire Seacoast and as a senior minister of a prominent downtown church, I have built-in visibility that has drawn me into relationship with the black community in ways I never expected.

From my early days in town, I have been invited to speak at and attend events in the black community. I have been asked to be part of panel discussions on current social issues and the church and participate in civic occasions recognizing and honoring black history and present-day achievements. My church has also hosted events with the black community. Ironically, moving to a community like Portsmouth has opened up new possibilities for ministry in and with the black community that were hard to come by in the San Francisco Bay Area, where I served previously. Saying yes to opportunities as they arose and building relationships in town has enabled me to enter into a rich realm of ministry that feeds and fuels me.

While many congregants are aware of this aspect of my ministry in Portsmouth, I don't believe any are aware of its extent or what it means to me. I have not hesitated to pull an all-nighter to write a talk or show up at an event in the black community even though I was sick. That said, I have prioritized my ministry with the black community well behind my obligations to my own congregation, even though it infuses my ministry with a spiritual vitality that congregants feel and appreciate. I would like to enter into deeper dialogue with lay leaders about the spiritual centrality of this piece of my ministry. I'm not sure yet when or how to do that.

Finding a Voice

Worship, preaching in particular, is deeply relational, emerging from the relationship between the preacher, the community she serves, the religious tradition, and the holy. For that reason, the community has an enormous impact on a preacher's emerging voice over time. Some aspects of good preaching and good worship are common to any setting—the preacher's capacity to listen to the people she serves, whoever they are; the preacher's ability to discern wisdom and inspiration in the source traditions with which she works; and having the tools to connect the message to the people. But there are also significant particularities that arise out of the community a person is serving—different cultures, different metaphors, different shared language, and different expectations. A preacher learns how to use stories, delivery, rhythms, metaphors, and music that touch the hearts and minds of the particular people she serves.

Preparing for ministry in black communities has included a number of elements. Personal experience in these communities has of course been crucial. In seminary, I took a number of courses with a focus on African-American experience. These involved a number of the offices of ministry. I took a homiletics course on preaching without notes at the Graduate Theological Union's American Baptist seminary. I took an ecojustice course, looking at environmental issues with a lens that highlighted racial and economic aspects of environmentalism. I took a course on Islam and the African-American experience, a course that explored American Muslim practices as acts of resistance in an oppressive social context. I took a pastoral care course, which emphasized culturally competent pastoral care and systemic thinking. I took courses on the works of Howard Thurman, on womanist writers, and on the thought of Martin Luther King Jr. and Malcolm X. While only one of these courses was specifically about preaching, all have shaped my ministry and, therefore, my preaching. They shape the way I approach various topics and the source material from which I draw. They have given me tools that enable my ministry to be relevant to a broader range of experience.

In addition, I have found that cultural and religious literacy/ fluency is vital to effective ministry in any setting. Whatever my personal theology, it helps to be culturally literate about black communities. For me, that has meant study and building relationships. It has also meant personal work to come to terms with my own identity and social location within the black community.

It matters to speak the religious language of the black church, which is largely influenced by Christianity, Islam, and other religious practices of the African diaspora. Ministry in most UU settings requires only minimal knowledge of Christianity and Islam, let alone other African spiritual traditions. Effective ministry in black settings requires it. That doesn't mean that a black Humanist minister needs to pretend to be Christian or Muslim. It simply means that she needs to have worked through her relationships with those faith traditions, to have arrived at a relationship that feels relatively comfortable. And it means that she needs to know about the black church and have some understanding of Christian scripture, theology, and practices.

This is true on a cultural level as well. The black community is very diverse. To move easily in black communities as a minister, I need to have found my own place in the community, and then learn to relate to a broader range of people within it.

On my mother's side, I come from a long line of middle-class black folks from the Northeast. The values, language, and heritage of that part of the black community are rich, and I cherish them. That community also has a shadow side that I have explored. I personally grew up in a number of predominantly white communities, and black folks who came up that way have particular experiences, patterns of challenges in identity formation. Many, but not all, African-American Unitarian Universalists fall into this category. My father's family were transplanted Southerners who moved from South Carolina to Ohio, to a small black community at the edge of a college town. Most of the people there had strong ties to the South, with rural ways of living. Economically, most were living closer to the edge of poverty. The people I came to know in Ohio were, for the most part, part of the

---

I'm a cradle UU and I was raised in a White family, so I don't have a community outside that I've had a connection to. A lot of UUs of color in our movement who were raised by White people have serious identity issues; we don't fit in anywhere. The piece that's challenging me the most is that I don't fit in here either. The hardest thing is when you don't fit into the people of color around you. And so I stand outside again. I'm not a theist. I'm not Christian. I'm not part of a Black community. I'm not coming from somewhere else. I am here as a UU because there is no place else to be, because I'm multiracial, multicultural, multi-everything. And that's what Unitarian Universalism has been for me, and that's why I love it. It's also why I resent it. But it's also why it has saved me, because it said, "You are welcome here," even if it doesn't always mean it.

REV. DR. KRISTEN HARPER

Great Migration of black people out of the South in the twentieth century. My grandparents, uncles, and aunts mostly moved there after World War II to find greater economic and educational opportunity. My father was the first person in my family and on his block to go to college. In the mix, on my mother's side, is a contingent of West Indians (Jamaican and Barbadian) who settled in Harlem in the early twentieth century. They were also well educated, came from a position of prominence in the West Indies, and experienced the Harlem Renaissance in the United States. These three distinct locations in the black community have formed me. They are my home base in the black community. Each of these locations has gifts and shadow sides. And there are whole swaths of the black community to which I have had little exposure, except indirectly or in popular culture. I have minimal and indirect experience of Southern black culture and inner-city black culture. I have minimal exposure to the world of the black upper class. When I enter these realms, I often feel out of my element.

There was a time when I felt illegitimate in my black identity and ill at ease in certain settings. I was easily triggered when someone (white, black, or other) "pulled my black card" because of my musical tastes or the way I dressed. That is no longer the case. I feel comfortable with who I am, even as I continue to grow.

———

In my congregation, which is vastly White, almost all the people of color call me Reverend Bill or Pastor, and it just makes my heart feel good whenever they do that.

REV. DR. WILLIAM SINKFORD

When Worlds Collide

Up to this point, most of the most challenging moments in my formation as a preacher have been when my worlds collided on a large scale. Three situations come to mind.

The first was at our arrival. There were questions about what my husband Chris and I wanted to be called, Rev. Lauren and Rev. Chris, or Lauren and Chris. This was a culturally laden conversation. Early on, in a sermon in which I spoke about the African notion of *ubuntu*, I broached the subject:

> The spirit of *ubuntu* runs deep in African American culture. I love to be greeted with, "I see you, my sister," which I sometimes am in the black community. Even in the way we greet one another, there is power to lift one another up.
>
> I am reminded of this because I've had a lot of conversations lately about what Chris and I wish to be called— Rev. Lauren and Rev. Chris, or just Lauren and Chris. Unitarian Universalists tend to be pretty informal. We're blue-jeans-at-church, first-name-basis kind of people, for the most part. That informality is really important to a lot of folks because it stands for something. It marks the church as a place set apart from social stratification. It's a way of saying that when we look at one another, we see *people*, not degrees or titles or marital status.
>
> In the African-American church, where I spent much of my childhood, that spirit of interpersonal respect is the same, but it shows up differently. Black churches tend to be quite formal. I'm forty years old, but I still call the elders in my grandmother's church Mr. and Mrs., and I call the minister Rev. Roberson. Even when I call people by their first names, there's usually something that comes first. Geneva Cannon, who lives next door, is Aunt Jenny,

and Luther, who cuts my grandmother's grass, is Mr. Luther to me.

The black church emerged in the American South, where black people were highly visible, and also invisible in significant ways. In my grandparents' day, it was customary for white people to call black people by their first names—and it was acceptable to use generic names like Tom or Mary [regardless of a person's given name]. Black people were expected to address white people formally. It was a daily way of reinforcing the power structures of the Jim Crow South and belittling the humanity of black people.

So when we came to church, we dressed up. We greeted one another formally. And that formality had the same purpose as the informality in many Unitarian Universalist congregations. It was a way of saying, "I see you" and "I am here," a ritual of acknowledgment, respect, and recognition.

I let the congregation know that they could address us formally or informally, as they pleased. But I was grateful for the opportunity to explicate different cultural interpretations of that simple choice.

That service was not about blackness, per se. It was actually the launch of our small group ministry program for the year, a chance to get people excited about small groups and encourage them to sign up. The service wasn't about blackness, but it drew on several black sources—from the African concept of *ubuntu* to the ideas of theologian Howard Thurman and writer Ralph Ellison.

I was genuinely comfortable with whatever choice my congregants made about what to call me. That said, I did find myself mildly uncomfortable when we hosted a Juneteenth event at the church. We provided the space, but the event was organized by the Seacoast African-American Cultural Center. The event organizers and many of the participants were black. Many of them included my title when they spoke to me, and they relieved me of mundane duties when they saw me doing them (helping to cart tables, moving trash cans, and so on). Respect for the office of ministry is just a cultural norm in many parts of the black community. Members of my congregation were also present, many of whom simply don't think that way about ministers. Their choice isn't a product of the racial difference between us. It's just a cultural norm. But the reality was that the cultural overlay meant that white people were treating me differently than black people, in a way that felt mildly uncomfortable. I know my congregants and their respect for me. I was concerned about how our guests would interpret their way of interacting with me and what conclusions they might draw about how welcome black people were in the space.

On a second occasion, I pulled together a blessing service for the almost-complete African Burying Ground memorial just a block and a half from the church. There had been a decade-long effort to build a memorial on an African burying ground that had previously been paved under a Portsmouth city street. For that morning, I had invited two local African-American ministers to help lead worship. Rev. Robert Thompson is the minister of Phillips Chapel at Exeter Academy nearby. Rev. Lillian Buckley pastored a small Christian church north of Portsmouth. Each of us offered a brief homily. Rev. Thompson and Rev. Buckley both sang as well. My husband, Chris, offered the prayer.

I was nervous. It was the first time I had led worship in a UU setting with mostly black colleagues. I was not nervous that the congregation would react negatively to having black ministers in the pulpit. I was nervous because many Unitarian Universalists have a conflicted relationship to Christianity. I wanted to invite my colleagues to share the day, and I hoped the congregation would extend them the courtesy of respecting their right to preach from their own traditions, but I did not know how they would respond.

*I so relate to, but haven't known how to talk about,
being terrified when organizing a worship service that's
related to core aspects of who I am. You would think that
it's easy for someone of Hindu heritage to lead a service
about Hinduism. However, it causes so much stress. It
also causes me a great deal of stress to have colleagues of
color in the pulpit with me, to have other Asian spiritual
leaders or African-American spiritual leaders with me in
worship. I love doing it, but it's terrifying and stressful at
the same time. Part of it is that I'm allowing myself to be
seen in a way that's even more full and rich. So what
happens if that's rejected? What if that deeper level of
vulnerability is not seen? What if it's not received in
ways that are gracious? That would hurt. It's almost
easier to hide behind a mask and pretend I'm White,
even though I'm not. Then there are those times when I
take off the mask and say, "Okay, by the way, I'm
Hindu. Maybe we could have a Diwali service. And by
the way, I'm not White in our culture. I want to invite in
some non-White colleagues in the local area to worship
with us." It's necessary and important, and for those
who receive it well, it's a beautiful, rewarding thing
to do. But it's hard because of the possibility of
rejection and of not being seen.*

REV. MANISH MISHRA-MARZETTI

Leading worship with my colleagues, hearing their voices, and receiving the gift of their word and song in my sanctuary as we came together to bless the burying ground meant so much to me. It went well, despite some difficult comments here and there. And welcoming them into my home sanctuary brought more of who I am as a minister into the sanctuary as well. I doubt that many in the congregation had any inkling how important that day was for me. It was terrifying and rewarding. It was a risk, and I'm grateful to have taken it.

The slow work of unpacking our baggage around Christianity and Islam as faith traditions, developing comfort in engaging with Christian scripture and people, has everything to do with my capacity to be in relationship with my congregation and black communities so that I don't feel like a bridge stretched thin between disparate worlds. This doesn't mean I wish for my congregation to become more Christian or Muslim, just that I wish for my congregation (and our denomination) to grow more flexible in its willingness to hear about and learn from those sources of wisdom, to grow in courtesy in relation to the Christians and Muslims within and outside our congregations.

My worlds collided especially during the upheaval around police brutality in Ferguson, Cleveland, New York, and other places around the country in the past few years. I had deep personal feelings about these events. I was angry and sad about the violence that is visited on black communities, and frustrated at the facile ways that violence is minimized in mainstream culture. As a minister, it felt important to address the issues in worship. But I didn't want to. On a personal level, I wanted to retreat and make sense of it all on my own or with the black community. I did not feel spiritually ready to take up ministry to and with my congregation, even though I felt that it should be done. I felt that denial around racism in policing and public policy needed to be confronted, but I was already feeling angry, sad, and personally violated. I did not have the emotional bandwidth to handle the backlash that often comes after speaking on one of these subjects. And it would have been difficult if the intensity of my feeling became grounds for minimizing or sidestepping the underlying issues, which happens a lot in conversations about race. You hear things like: "It would be a lot easier to hear what you have to say if you weren't so angry." Also, because I am one of fewer than five black people in a congregation of almost five hundred, and because I am a minister, I sometimes become the person with whom a large number of people feel safe sorting through their beliefs and feelings. I had no desire to be a lightning rod. I had no desire to be the foil against which people sorted out their feelings and beliefs. This is always a part of ministry, and I accept it most of the time, but the dynamic is extended by an order of magnitude when you're a black person raising issues of race in a predominantly white community.

A number of strategies helped me navigate this tension. First, I do not minister alone. I co-minister with my husband and with a dedicated and thoughtful band of lay leaders. Chris and some lay leaders were motivated and skilled enough to take the lead. This allowed me latitude to participate in ministry to the congregation but make choices about how to engage in ways that felt affirming on a personal level. My husband preached the first sermon that touched on the issues. I offered the children's story and the prayer that morning.

On another occasion, around the time of the fiftieth anniversary of the Selma marches, I crafted a worship service with a lay leader and in conjunction with a commemorative march organized by our social justice associates. Three reflections were offered that day. One member of the congregation, Kimberly, described her experience as a white woman finding a way through the issues at hand, making sense of the situation, and discerning how to respond. She is a gifted speaker, and she spoke from a place of shared identity with most of the congregation. I spoke, as well, from a more historical perspective. Finally, Rev. Brad Greeley, who is also a member of the congregation, offered a reflection at the start of our commemorative walk. Brad is a white man who participated in the events at Selma in 1965. He spoke eloquently and passionately, placing our contemporary struggles in historical perspective. Kimberly and Brad spoke beautifully from their own social location, and I spoke openly from my own. I was released from the responsibility of ministry to white people in relationship to a black issue. I could speak from my own experience, while helping to ensure that we collectively attended to the needs of the congregation. I am called to minister at the intersection of Unitarian Universalism and black communities, but I chafe at a dynamic that comes up frequently in Unitarian Universalist settings. There is a constant pull to minister to white people about their relationships with people of color. Much of our antiracism work has primarily been about transforming the hearts and minds of white people. Ironically, it has consistently placed white people at the center. I cherish the privilege of ministry to all people, but the center of my call to ministry is to and with people of color.

During that first service after Ferguson, the one my husband preached, I offered the poem "Ka'ba" by Amiri Baraka, which was given to me by a member of the congregation, as part of the prayer. It speaks to the spiritual journey of black people. I was grateful to be able to participate in this way—to speak in the first-person plural in the service with the black community as a referent.

Looking back at my formation as a preacher, I am grateful for the many ways to grow into the ministry to which I feel called. As I look ahead, I see more opportunities for growth. I can say yes to public ministry in the black community when opportunities arise. I want to continue to deepen and extend my relationships to both parts of the community in which I move easily and to parts of the community in which I feel less comfortable. I can soak up and enjoy the rich cultural heritage of black music, literature, academic resources, food, history, and more—so that I may draw on it as a resource in ministry. I want to study the religious traditions of the African diaspora, especially Christianity and Islam. I will find ways to support my congregation in developing intercultural competency, including its capacity to engage with Christianity and Christians, Islam, and Muslims. I want to continue to learn about my own black roots and deepen my own black community. I can collaborate with people of other racial and religious identities in order to learn from difference and free myself to speak from my own experience. I want to grow in the capacity to lead multivocal worship. I will watch for unexpected opportunities. Very often, at least one of these routes of growth is available. The journey continues.

RESPONSE TO LAUREN SMITH
Rev. Dr. Susan Newman Moore

I F I WROTE A GUIDE for religious professionals of color considering a call at a predominantly White church setting—especially a UU church—I'd entitle it "What You Need to Know Before You Go." After six years as the associate minister of All Souls Church, Unitarian, Washington D.C., I want to encourage folk to know why they are going to their place of calling and to find UU professionals of color and White allies to be their guides.

———

Can we prioritize serving our own communities as much as we serve the broader institution? We don't have time at the end of the day to do it, and I think we have been misprioritizing our time as a coalition-building community writ large. Let's go fifty-fifty. I'm not saying forget all our national commitments, but how do we help each other reshape this paradigm?

REV. SOFIA BETANCOURT

———

My ministry was birthed in the womb of the Black Christian church. It has been visible and invisible for more than forty years because of my gender, age, and race. I began preaching when I was fifteen and was licensed by the Baptist church at the age of nineteen. As a seminarian at Howard University School of

Divinity, I needed a church for my internship, but there weren't any Black Baptist pulpits open to a woman in Washington D.C. in 1979 except on Women's Day. Peoples Congregational United Church of Christ (UCC)—a Black church—hired me as their seminarian. The UCC, though predominantly White, has a number of churches that are Latinx, American Indian, African American, Asian, and Pacific Islander. I was ordained in 1983—the seventh Black woman ordained in the UCC and the first Black woman ordained by a mainline denomination in the District of Columbia.

For the next twenty-seven years, I served in various ministerial capacities—hospital and college chaplain, associate and senior minister, executive at faith-based nonprofits, religious advisor to the mayor, adjunct faculty, and author. Having served at a Black UCC church in Atlanta, Georgia, I returned to Washington D.C. in 2000 to care for my mother, who was experiencing health problems. I was now landlocked for choices of available churches in the area. In 2010, while serving as policy director at the Religious Coalition for Reproductive Choice, I was invited to preach at All Souls Church, Unitarian, for Neighborhood Justice Sunday. After preaching, I received a roaring standing ovation. Rev. Robert Hardies, the senior minister, leaned over and said, "I've been here eleven years and haven't gotten that kind of response. When White people stand up after a sermon they're usually going home."

A few weeks later he called me and said, "Susan, I know you have a full-time job, but we'll pay you to be in worship with us on Sunday." I asked Rob, "What do you really need?" They were seeking an associate minister and needed an interim. I missed parish ministry, so I interviewed and was hired as the interim. I'd fallen in love with the people and the ministry. The next year I was called as the associate minister, a surprising outcome since some expressed disappointment that I was not a Humanist or

Unitarian. This was my first indication that my cultural challenge would be not just about race but also about my faith.

Working in a predominantly White church setting was not new to me. I'd worked on the national staff and in parishes of the United Church of Christ and the American Baptist Churches, USA. The challenge I faced was that the Black churches were not ready to call a woman as the senior minister—unless they had an emergency situation—and the White churches, which often had White women as senior ministers, were not yet comfortable with a Black woman as the senior minister. All Souls is 80-percent White and 20-percent people of color. Some of the Black members have been there since Rev. David Eaton, the first Black pastor in the Unitarian Universalist Association, was called as senior minister in 1969.

I am a progressive, Christian minister who preaches the radical, inclusive love of God, I am a straight ally for the LGBTQ community, and my ministry has always "pushed the envelope" in the Christian church. So I figured that since the Unitarian Universalist church was progressive about issues of human sexuality, reproductive justice, and antiracism, I would be a natural fit. I've worked in ecumenical and interfaith contexts all my life. So, if All Souls wanted to be intentionally multiracial and multicultural, I was willing to help bring that about.

I was willing to be the canary in the coal mine. Early coal mines did not have ventilation systems, so legend has it that miners would bring a caged canary into new coal seams. Canaries are especially sensitive to methane and carbon monoxide, which made them ideal for detecting any dangerous gas buildups. As long as the bird kept singing, the miners knew their air supply was safe. A dead canary signaled unseen danger in the air—for the canary and for the miners.

When I arrived at All Souls, my first experience of culture shock was being called Susan. Unlike Lauren, who said, "I was

*A perfect storm is coming around the behavior of congregants
and the lack of accountability around that behavior. It has
been brought to light by what people who are studying for the
ministry understand from either their internships or their field
education and their conversations with those of us who have
been in the parish. It's not going to be pretty. For those of us
who are people of color, this started earlier. We started getting
out of the parish a lot earlier because of the experiences we
were having with congregants, and race was a huge factor
around that, but it was also the larger issue of entitlement. We
have begun to address our inability to divert behavior that
basically wrecks ministers' careers and breaks their hearts. The
heartbreak part is not a joke. I know very few ministers of
color whose hearts have not been broken, even those who have
stayed in the parish. Many ministers don't talk about it. People
of color are more likely to talk about it, but as in many things,
people don't listen to what we have to say. As a result, I have
this horrible feeling that congregations are going to be
increasingly surprised at how hard it will be for them to get a
minister once people begin to retire in even larger numbers
than they do right now. So one reason antiracism work and
what we call counter-oppressive work is so important is that it
teaches us early what people need to know. It's information.
It's a heads-up around a whole host of things that people don't
pay attention to because it's us talking and we don't get heard.*

REV. ROSEMARY BRAY MCNATT

———

genuinely comfortable with whatever choice my congregants made about what to call me," I wasn't. For more than thirty-five years I've been called Reverend or Dr. Newman (I became Dr. Newman Moore when I married in 2013). Suddenly people I don't know are calling me Susan. In the Black church one would never call the minister by her first name; it's seen as disrespectful. It would be like me calling my mother Lillian.

Many ministers of color are the first in our families to receive a doctorate. We've worked hard to earn it, and unlike White people, we do not have the privilege or luxury to allow someone to not recognize our educational achievements. Calling someone by their first name without permission also gives the false impression of an intimacy that does not exist yet.

My next cultural conflict was in the pulpit. As a Christian minister from the Black church, I was used to preaching from a biblical text. In the UU church, the reading for the sermon is usually a poem. I'd never heard of the poet Mary Oliver before coming to All Souls. Her poems are for Unitarian Universalists like the writings of the apostle Paul for Christians. Whenever I preached, before I arrived home I'd received emails about my sermon. Folk were complaining because I used a text from the Bible instead of a reading from a nontheistic source. I gradually found myself compromising my style of preaching. When I was scheduled to preach, I wrote three sermons. The first was written as I was inspired by the Spirit. The second was edited for the UU ear, and the third was watered down so I'd still be employed after the benediction. I did not feel free to bring my whole self to the preaching moment. I wasn't preaching in my authentic voice. It was only when I became angry about some injustice, like the murder of Eric Garner or Sandra Bland, that I preached uninhibitedly—not caring whether my message was liked or not.

After forty years as a revered preacher and homiletics teacher and after having several of my sermons published in books, I was insulted. My sermons were constantly being scrutinized and criticized by some White congregants. I later learned that for many Unitarian Universalists, it is a spiritual practice to dissect and analyze the sermon—often immediately after worship at the church. I felt like a woman who has endured hours of labor and birthed a child into the world hearing someone say my baby looks odd. For one who is unfamiliar with this type of response to a minister's sermon, it comes across as disrespectful and doubtful of the minister's abilities.

I remember the very moment when my preaching at All Souls changed. It was Sunday, January 20, 2013. That weekend was not only the Martin Luther King Jr. holiday Sunday but also President Barack Obama's second inauguration. Try as I might, I had difficulty writing my sermon. My topic was "It's Morning Time," and my reading was an excerpt from Dr. Maya Angelou's poem "On the Pulse of Morning." This was one of the few times I did not have difficulty finding a poem to go with the message.

I had my introduction. I had my first point and a supporting illustration. I knew where I wanted to go with the sermon, but the middle part kept eluding me. On Friday night, I called my beloved friend Rev. Dr. Jeremiah Wright Jr. I told him my problem. He said, "Sis, what are you preaching about?" I shared what I'd written. He then asked, "What are you *not* saying?" I told him about my frustrations that even though President Obama was beginning his second term in office, and it was "morning time" for Black people, it was not nine A.M.—but more like a minute past midnight. Jeremiah said, "That's what you need to preach."

I was frustrated because African Americans had not experienced greater socioeconomic justice in the past few years, and I was also annoyed and discouraged about things at the church. Jeremiah's words rang true to what had been growing in my heart at All Souls. I was becoming disheartened as a preacher. It was wearing on me to know that my racial culture as an African American was welcomed but my religious culture as a Christian was not.

My racial identity, like so many whose ancestors were brought here in chains as slaves, is tied to my faith in God—a God who Black liberation theologian Dr. James H. Cone calls "the God of the oppressed." The same way Yahweh is revealed in the history of the Exodus of the oppressed Jews enslaved in Egypt, God's presence is revealed in the liberation of Black people from social and political bondage. The faith of Black people throughout history has been the common thread of our fight for justice and freedom. The civil rights movement was midwifed in the basements of Black churches throughout the South. Our civil rights leaders—men, women, and children—praying, marching, singing, and going to jail together with the words of scripture on their lips and prayers in their hearts.

All people of color are not Christian, nor are all civil and human rights advocates people of faith. Yet one cannot ignore the historical and powerful presence of a theocentric catalyst for African-American people fighting for justice in America. Even as I felt welcomed as an African-American minister, whispered voices encouraged me to keep my faith invisible and muted.

When I first came to the church, a man walked up to me and let me know that he was an atheist and did not believe as I did. On that Martin Luther King Jr. Sunday, three years later, he shook my hand and said, "The preacher that preached today is who I want to hear from now on." It was a wonderful affirmation. When he heard me boldly preach in my authentic voice, he gladly received the message. He did not see his projection of a Christian preacher; he saw me proclaiming God's justice and love, bringing my whole self to the preaching moment.

I'm in my sixth year at the church, and I am just beginning to feel comfortable preaching the first sermon I write. I am thankful for those members—Black and White elders of the church—who have been guides and allies. They've encouraged me along the way. It is because of them I can possibly see myself pastoring a Unitarian Universalist Church and truly lifting up the historical theist roots in our tradition.

In *Footprints of a Dream*, Dr. Howard Thurman writes, "The movement of the Spirit of God in the hearts of men often calls them to act against the spirit of their times or causes them to anticipate a spirit which is yet in the making. In a moment of dedication, they are given wisdom and courage to dare a deed that challenges and to kindle a hope that inspires."

Representing

Rev. Manish Mishra-Marzetti

THE SIMPLE ACT of being a Unitarian Universalist of color is fraught with symbolism and meaning that far exceeds the individual life story of any one of us. It means representing, for many, the hope and dream that Unitarian Universalism may one day more proportionately hold the racial and cultural diversity that exists within our nation. It means belonging to an intentionally pluralist theological tradition that struggles deeply with its relationship to the cultural, racial, and class-based aspects of genuine pluralism. It means navigating the perceptions held by some of our Unitarian Universalist kinfolk that we have an easy time being UU because our mere presence is so lauded and celebrated, at least on the surface. It means holding deep pain at the recognition that, ultimately, our denomination and its congregations reflect the same patterns, behaviors, and attitudes around race and culture that permeate our society at large; we are not magically further along simply because of our liberal theology. It means that, at times, I have had my personal experiences of racism, discrimination, and invisibility actively negated by otherwise good-hearted UUs. It means that, like other UUs of color, I have struggled at times with simultaneously holding optimism, pessimism, anger, joy, sadness, and gratitude in my heart. At times I have held these tensions and contradictions well, and at other times I have not. At times, I have given in to the anger, sadness, and frustration; at other times hope and possibility have buoyed me. Learning how to live well with this hodgepodge of intense realities has required arriving at a clearer and healthier relationship with the call to "represent."

My experience in Unitarian Universalism is not dissimilar to that of many UUs of color: As someone who came into the faith as an adult, my arrival at a UU congregation was greeted with warmth and enthusiasm. In my late twenties, I happened to stumble upon All Souls Church, Unitarian, in Washington D.C. without any prior awareness of All Souls' long-standing commitment to racial, cultural, and theological diversity. At that time, the congregation was reeling from the painful dismissal of its most recent senior minister and was just entering a church year that was heavily driven by lay-led ministry. Joining the congregation during this time of transition, I was rapidly invited into leadership. "You should preach!" I was told. At that time, when I was serving as a diplomat with the U.S. Foreign Service, public speaking was both easy and enjoyable for me. To my chagrin, the invitation was enthusiastically followed up with, "You should preach about Hinduism!" I was attending a UU congregation to form and deepen a sense of my connection to Unitarian Universalism, not necessarily to educate others about Hinduism. However, I recognized that for many of my friends within the congregation, I was the only person of Hindu background they knew well. In addition, it felt important to support our UU commitment to theological diversity; I wanted our congregation to feel like it could honor and learn from the Hindu faith. Thus, I chose to represent Hinduism for my UU kin.

I subsequently wrestled deeply with figuring out what I would want to meaningfully share with majority-culture UUs about Hinduism while also being honest about its shortcomings. While this process of revisiting my faith of origin was unexpected, it did help me go back to my theological roots and reclaim those parts that had always resonated with me. I began learning how to navigate and integrate these two disparate aspects of myself and share that spiritual journey with others. In essence, the call to represent Hinduism for other UUs put me on the road to being a better Unitarian Universalist and a better Hindu.

But no sooner was my initial foray into preaching complete and received with rave reviews, than I was invited to preach again: "We hope you'll share even more with us about Hinduism!" I discovered that it's possible to be both honored and perturbed at the same time.

Over time, those invitations to preach gradually guided me toward seminary, to Harvard Divinity School, where I remember being absolutely shocked to find myself the only non-White person in the first UU-related course I took. Coming from All Souls, where the congregational demographics more closely reflected the diversity of our country, I had no idea that most UU congregations did not look and feel like All Souls. Throughout that entire first class session, I kept thinking, *why aren't we talking about* this? *How can everybody just keep going on as if this utter lack of diversity is normal, as if this is okay?* My confusion and pain led me that first semester to a trusted friend and mentor, who gently steered me toward DRUUMM (Diverse Revolutionary Unitarian Universalist Multicultural Ministries), our national UU people of color organization. Within DRUUMM I began exploring and learning what it might mean for me to be a UU "of color" (a new concept to me at the time). Within DRUUMM, I found others who had wrestled, and continued to wrestle, just as I was with the reality of Unitarian Universalist homogeneity. The sense of supportive connection I found in this UU community led me to gradually deepen my personal commitment to the organization, serving at ever higher levels of leadership and eventually as president.

In parallel to my journey within DRUUMM, I was increasingly invited into new and widely different leadership settings within our denomination. Often these were areas with which I had little experience or background, but that lack of experience didn't seem to bother the folks doing the inviting. From my end, I was flattered to be asked. I recognized that often these invitations

*I know a lot of people who have been largely influenced
and fallen in love with our supposedly multicultural
congregations led by White male ministers, and that model
does not serve us. I'm seeing people of color, and teens,
and young adults attracted to that model. But then those
people of color who move into ministerial training don't
have enough mentors of color who can help them navigate
the system. That's an area where we really need to do some
work. When I needed a mentor in preliminary fellowship,
I had to ask for a dispensation to get a person of color.
Nobody came to me and said, "You need the option of
having a mentor of color. Here's a list." Nobody said that.
I made that for myself, and that is not right. That is too
much to ask me to do for myself, when it was so obvious
that people of color in Unitarian Universalist ministry
need the option of a mentor of color.*

REV. NATALIE MAXWELL FENIMORE

————

came to me because some group, committee, or institution wanted
to be sure they were including the perspectives of people of color
in their work or planning. Heck, if they thought that I was a person of color they wanted to work with, perhaps I could do some
good! Perhaps I could even help bring about the changes it was
so clear to me our faith needed to make. The ego strokes of being
asked to serve led to a bit of hubris on my end; maybe if all these
folks thought I was "important," perhaps I was, in fact, important
enough to bring about the changes that UUs of color needed. Thus,
I chose to represent in our broader UU world as a person of color.

*I'm thinking about the power of positioning the UU
leader of Color. All of a sudden one day you wake up
and you are all over the national stage, and you are
the hottest thing since sliced bread. But it's going to be
someone else before you look around. As difficult as it
is to move forward through our ministries as
Unitarian Universalist leaders, we need to recognize
the frailties, the vulnerabilities. We have to take a
deep breath and decide yes or no, I'm going to move
forward or I'm going to hold back. This is a tension
we each live with every day.*

REV. DR. HOPE JOHNSON

The Dangers of Representing

Representing has benefits. The pull to represent at the regional or denominational level can be sharply counterbalanced at the local level, particularly in congregational settings, where the expectation for a parish minister of color can be exactly the opposite. We are almost always the first ministers of color to be serving the congregations where our ministry takes us. These communities harbor some measure of anxiety that we might be passionate about diversity and that we might impose that passion on the congregation in some way. Clergy of color have been driven out of congregations and pegged as single-issue ministers or as ministers who focus on social justice to the detriment of other needs. Just as perilously, any conversation about the fact that the ministries we lead are cross-cultural is viewed as somehow self-serving or self-absorbed; we are the ones who most starkly notice the ways in which we are traversing a cross-cultural landscape in what we're building between our congregations and ourselves, and any attempt to name, talk about, or work with the cross-cultural aspects of that reality is deemed unnecessary. We are essentially whitewashed. Any and all ethnic, racial, and cultural differences between us and our congregations are painted over, and if we, as clergy of color, name or bring attention to the fact that something is being missed or lost, we run the risk of becoming "the problem"—we are the ones highlighting difference or divergence. The very qualities that place us in demand in the unpaid, volunteer circles of the denomination make us anxiety-producing prospects in the paid work of congregational ministry. This reality is borne out in the statistics: There are very few long-settled congregational ministers of color, our rates of settlement are lower than for our White peers, and when we do get settlements, the well-worn pattern has been that those settlements tend to be shorter in duration than those of our White colleagues.

Acknowledging these stark realities, one could argue that there are some benefits to representing in the areas where we are often encouraged to provide leadership, at the regional and denominational levels. For one thing, it can be great for the ego; believing that the accolades, the praise, the invitations, and the

---

I serve in a congregation where I can't put up a Black Lives Matter banner. So what does that say about my congregation? What does that say about me as a minister? I mean, does it look like I think I'm so Caribbean that I don't really need to care about my African-American siblings?

REV. DR. HOPE JOHNSON

71

If you piss off the wrong person, what's going to happen?
Who's not afraid of getting fired? I was in a conversation
with an intern minister who said she had to be careful
because at some point she was going to see the
Ministerial Fellowship Committee. I wonder what
that does to Unitarian Universalism as a faith.

AISHA HAUSER

———————

access to power are about you *yourself* feels great. Even if one allows that such openings may be presenting themselves primarily or even exclusively because of identity, it is still quite easy to justify buying into this gestalt for the sake of "the good that one can do" through the access and roles being offered. After all, someone is going to get invited to be on that board, committee, group, program—why not you? At least as self-aware persons of color, we can use those roles and that access to make things better for others. Right? Maybe.

But maybe not. It depends. More specifically, it depends on one's headspace around all this. In my case, after several years of high-profile access and roles in which I certainly did some measure of good, other troubling issues started becoming clearer. First, I began to appreciate that I was serving institutional needs more than the needs of any particular group or higher cause that I might have hoped to serve. When our UU institutions ask, want, or expect us as people of color to represent (whether implicitly or outright), we are allowing the institution to pursue, in part, a feel good approach. It feels good to our collective institutions to have nonmajority culture individuals in key roles (on boards, search committees, task forces, etc.), and it feels good to us, as people of color, to be included in such important tasks. But this feel good approach has many deep costs embedded in it. The ability to repeatedly turn to the few people of color who are in our congregations and denomination can keep us UUs from building authentic relationships with communities of color. If I represent what Hindus think, believe, say, and do, what need is there for any UU group to go out and actually develop an ongoing, long-term relationship with a Hindu temple community? If our relatively few African-American UUs are the only folks we engage with to understand the needs and struggles of Black America, we UUs can feel like we've done our job and never bother actually forming meaningful, continuing relationships with Black institutions and communities. We UUs of color who buy into representing can wind up being complicit with systems and patterns of behavior

———

It's important and powerful to talk about the water that we swim in, the current that we swim against, because quite often it's invisible to others. In this denomination that holds up the welcoming and loving and all this other wonderful stuff with words and concepts, we fail very miserably much too often in the practice. That dichotomy is important to name and prepare for. How to do it I don't know. Fortunately, I've had close mentors and friends and colleagues who pulled me down off the ceiling several times. There are gatekeepers. It got real clear to me that I wasn't the Black man I was supposed to be, coming through this process. The message was, "We don't know that we can control you, so we need you to understand we're in charge."

REV. WALTER LEFLORE

73

that value feel-good shortcuts over the harder work of forging truly transformative cross-cultural, cross-racial partnerships.

In addition, there is also a personal toll on us as UUs of color. Simply trying to keep up with all the places in which Unitarian Universalism would have us show up, if we could, can be exhausting. But here's the question that I never asked myself or anticipated: Having made the compromises and sacrifices that are necessary in order to represent, what happens when it feels like you're banging your head against a brick wall? What happens when the pace of institutional transformation feels snail-like in comparison to the personal sacrifices you have made? Never having considered this question, I found myself caught off guard by increasing levels of bitterness and frustration the longer that I was in national UU leadership. Unitarian Universalism was not changing, evolving, or growing at the pace at which I hoped it

———

I've had people search the whole building to find me because the Black family walked in and I have to say hello to them. I have to do that. And what is this congregation doing? How are they seeing that role that the professional of color has? How are they seeing the burden of that on people? I know it's difficult for people in parish ministry, but there's a particular burden when you see children and youth suffering and you see yourself and your role as being responsible for taking care of that in some way. As a professional association, I'd like for us to talk more about the resources that are available for people who find themselves in those situations.

REV. NATALIE MAXWELL FENIMORE

would, and yet the demand on my time and energy remained just as strong as ever. Why was I doing any of this, especially if there wasn't as strong a reciprocal commitment to the things that I and people in my communities needed? Exhausted, burned out, and disappointed, I dropped out of national UU leadership for a number of years, determined to focus instead on my local ministry.

Letting Go as a Way of Loving and Living More Deeply

That hiatus of about five years was one of the best things I could have done for myself. I stayed away from General Assembly. I stayed away from virtually any denominational or regional commitments. I focused on myself, my family, and my ministry. I decided that I could not personally change Unitarian Universalism, and I gave up any hope of being able to do so. That mental shift was incredibly helpful for me, and it reminded me of another similar time of letting go. When I was in my early twenties and had come out to my father as a gay man, we initially experienced a deep and painful wrestling between us: him wanting me to adapt or conform to his image of who I was supposed to be and me resisting his wants and needs with every breath in my body. It was only when my father completely let go—when he literally gave up on his expectations for our relationship—that he and I were able to circle back to one another and develop a new and healthier relationship.

Something similar has happened in my relationship with Unitarian Universalism. In giving up on trying to change Unitarian Universalism, I have accepted that Unitarian Universalism is a majority culture institution that may never be what I need, want, or desire it to be from my non-majority cultural perspective. And I'm okay with that. I haven't left. I'm still a committed and dedicated UU. I just realize that the religion I serve and love

After the success and decline of LUUNA (Latina/o Unitarian Universalist Networking Association), we have been invisible for the longest time. We got a second wave of notoriety because of immigration issues, but then the Black Lives Matter movement came and it's increasing. It should be so. It definitely needs to be so. But many, many Latinx young people are also dying in prison as victims of mass incarceration, and nobody cares or is in the fore. I feel the same thing is going to happen in our denomination again. I realized a long time ago that if we don't open our mouths and think and push and say, "We exist. Let's sing in Spanish. Let's do a poem by Pablo Neruda. Let's do something to show that we exist in the denomination," we are not mentioned. And we should be mentioned whenever we talk about oppression or discrimination and all of that, but it's not happening. And that's where I gave up.

REV. LILIA CUERVO

———

will likely never be what I wish it could be. That process of letting go has freed me to be more fully who I am. If Unitarian Universalism isn't going to change overnight to fit my ideal vision of the beloved community, well then I might as well be as fully and as wholly whoever and whatever I need to be in this life—we are both just going to have to love each other as is. That recognition and newer commitment has allowed me to step more fully into my passions and interests: studying Lakota spirituality, deepening my prayer life, exploring the spirituality of nature photography, and discovering the joys and challenges of what it means to be a dad, among other things. With the distance of several years and a new headspace, I have now been able to circle back and engage again with the larger UU movement. However, I am now the most selective that I have ever been about what I do and where I go. I do not say yes to something simply because I have been asked, no matter how important or prestigious the opportunity. I reflect on whether the opportunity is meaningful, whether it suits me, and whether it is something that expands my horizons in healthy ways. If it doesn't, someone else is welcome to it. I have found immense spiritual freedom, even expansiveness, in letting go of the lures that were once sucking me not only in but also dry.

Shirley Chisholm was asked why she, a Black woman, was running for president: "You don't have a chance. Why are you doing that?" And she said, "Because I am in love with the America that does not yet exist," and that's how Unitarian Universalism is also. I'm in love with the Unitarian Universalism that does not yet exist. But I have to hold both the love for that thing and the love for the reality. It does not yet exist. It will probably not exist in my lifetime. I don't think it will in that of my children, but I can't deny my love for it. You know, wanting to be there in that struggle. That's why I'm fighting.

REV. NATALIE MAXWELL FENIMORE

Challenges and Opportunity

Whether intentionally or not, we clergy of color are often left with an unambiguous and difficult message: "Represent to your heart's content at the regional or denominational levels, as long as you don't expect too much. But please, in the congregations you may serve, let us just pretend that you're White." This current paradigm, which is supported and reinforced in many ways, leaves unanswered the question of what, if anything, we may be able to do to nurture and further those clergy of color who are interested in congregational ministry. Unfortunately, our current ministerial environment is one in which many, if not most, UU congregations are unprepared for the cross-cultural aspects of calling a minister of color. Further, they are not only unaware of their lack of readiness in this regard but also actively resist such self-knowledge. We parish ministers of color are then left as the ones in the field needing to navigate professional landscapes that look and feel like this while somehow being simultaneously authentic and politic. In essence, we are the ones who wind up shouldering the responsibility for our congregation's cross-cultural decision to call us, simply because the congregations themselves lack the skills and insight needed to both see this and work with it. This is a challenging and stressful reality in a profession that, on good days, already has plenty of stress and challenge.

Simultaneously, we are also left with the question of tokenism at the regional and denominational levels. Can this faith that I love so dearly let go of its over-reliance on its relatively small number of non-majority race, non-majority culture UUs to teach, educate, and lead on issues that directly affect us? Can those in the majority take ownership of their need to educate themselves about issues that affect Asian American, African-American, and other communities? Better still, can the majority take ownership of our faith's deep need for ongoing, meaningful relationships

Our congregations are also passing. They often will accept the leadership of one, maybe two people of color, on a good day maybe four, and that is openness and diversity. They are often passing for those affluent, comfortable, upper-middle-class White people they may not be either.

REV. NATALIE MAXWELL FENIMORE

———

with communities of color at the local level? That, from my perspective, is where opportunity lies—not in a handful of us representing but rather in our collective UU engagement in building the local and national relationships that, over time, help prevent the desecration of mosques, help eradicate systems of violence against African-American communities, and help us show up as allies whenever and wherever we are needed by those struggling with oppression and discrimination. As often happens in genuine cross-cultural partnerships, we may find along the way that we, as a faith movement, are transformed by such relationships in ways that we cannot anticipate; we might discover that we are learning more about ourselves than we ever expected; we might even begin to see and hear our own UU religious leaders of color in new and different ways. Such is our promise, such is my prayer.

Response to
Manish Mishra-Marzetti
Rev. Rosemary Bray McNatt

T HANK YOU FOR YOUR reflections, Manish. I am grateful for
Manish's reflections in the previous essay. The contradictions
and dangers he speaks of are real. At the same time, reading them
took me back to my own introduction to Unitarian Universalism
and how different it was from his. I often joke with people that
I married into Unitarian Universalism, but it's not far from the
truth. I was nineteen and dating the man who later became my
husband when I was introduced to our faith. I went home with
Bob for spring break, and on Sunday morning, all people under
the McNatt roof went to church. That did not surprise me, but
the Community Church of New York did surprise me. Entering
the spare brick sanctuary, I saw on the walls enormous banners
with symbols of all the major faith traditions. I heard a sermon
by Donald Harrington, one of the great ministers of his generation. Most importantly of all, I went to coffee hour downstairs in
the assembly hall, where I was exposed to the two things that
surprised me most.

First was the incredible energy of the church's members. Some
of them were occupied at the membership table greeting visitors
who had come by themselves. Some of them were raising money
for Biafran relief; some were working on issues related to the
United Nations. Some were engrossed in a letter-writing cam-
paign on a New York City issue that I can't remember any details
about. Bob's parents were in the thick of things, and when they

weren't introducing me to their friends, and when their friends weren't exclaiming over Bob and telling me stories of how cute he was as a little boy (which I secretly *loved* hearing!), they were talking about church and the great issues of the day with incredible energy and love. I was impressed.

In those days, there was little discussion about the broader definitions of people of color that we now take for granted in our movement. All I knew was that Black people were everywhere I looked. They were older than I was, but I noticed some young people too. And they weren't just clumped into a little black knot at one end of the room all the time. They were fluid and engaged with White members. The Black and White members were friends with one another; they seemed to love one another.

Another decade passed before I became a member there in 1985, the year after I married Bob. What I loved about Unitarian Universalism was still there—the freedom to question and doubt that was lacking in the Catholic church of my childhood. What I loved about Community Church was still there—the commitment to social justice work of all kinds, the deep integration of its members. Black people there were clearly among the matriarchs and patriarchs of the church—that number included my in-laws. And all of them took me under their collective wing. I still have a memory of my first General Assembly in 1987 in Little Rock, Arkansas. I had rented a car and was acting as chauffeur to Mae Tabbanor, Winnie Norman (the first Black UUA trustee from our Metro New York District), and my mother-in-law, Gladys McNatt, who by then was the president of the International Association of Liberal Religious Women, the first Black woman to lead that group. I can't remember where we were going, only that each of them was sure of the right way to get there. It sounds awful, but it wasn't—these were powerful Unitarian Universalist women who had taken their place in our faith and were teaching me how to find my place and take it.

At the same time, General Assembly was where I first learned that all of Unitarian Universalism was not like Community Church. It was a rude awakening but not a fatal one, I suspect because I was surrounded by the Community Church cocoon. Delegates or not, Community Church people went to GA *en masse*—at least twenty people every year at that point, sometimes more. We sat together in plenary, spoke at the mics, participated in every aspect of GA. That's what we were taught to do.

I went to leadership school and became a member of the Church Council and joined the UUA Committee on Urban Concerns and Ministry. I joined every committee anyone asked me to join. I had fallen in love with church. At the same time, I began to experience what Manish discusses in his essay—the call to be present at every gathering about race, the request to be on every committee that any group could form. Because I was a writer, people wanted me to write on every subject under the sun. I simply didn't have the strength to do it all, but as a workaholic without children in the early years of our marriage, I had the

---

Every month, one of us was going to the UCC and the other of us was talking her out of it. This went on up until she died. By that time, we had sort of made our peace. Even then it was still a theological conversation between the two of us. It was like, if these people keep breaking out in hives every time I say Jesus, I don't know how much longer I can take this. But I guess I just refuse to give up what's mine. I'm just possessive. You can't have what's mine.

REV. ROSEMARY BRAY MCNATT

strength to do quite a lot. Then, as now, I believed you had to be in the room.

The one time I was tempted to withdraw from Unitarian Universalism, however, was for theological reasons. I was sick of anti-theist Unitarians who attempted to censor any honest expressions of faith. Years of the freedom that our faith provides had given me the room to return to God. Yet even my beloved congregation struggled with expressions of the sacred. With the help of a dear friend, Rebecca Parker, I stayed in our faith and grew in my connection to the holy.

By the time I had said yes to God's call in my life, by the time I had made the decision to go to seminary, I had made my peace with being a Black, theistic Unitarian Universalist. What was harder, however, was attempting to find my place among the men and women who would eventually become my colleagues. White men of a certain age, liberal at least in theory, behaved as though I were pledging for admission to a fraternity. In some ways I was. But where I had believed my embrace of the call to ministry would be met with rejoicing by others who had experienced it, I found instead indifference and, in a few cases, barely masked hostility. I often tell people that if our ministers had been the first people I met in Unitarian Universalism back then, I would be an Episcopalian today.

But I had a legacy I could count on that had nothing to do with my eventual colleagues. That was the previous generations of Black laywomen and laymen like Mae Tabbanor and Odella Washington and Helene Lightbourne and Maude Jenkins and Edd Lee and a band of others who discovered our faith because ministers like John Haynes Holmes and Donald Harrington and Dick Leonard were determined to walk their talk about what was then called integration. John Haynes Holmes was the one who made Isaac and Gladys McNatt welcome at Community Church in the 1940s. Whenever I visit my mother-in-law in North

I'm thinking about the ways we carve out space to find
ourselves in the language of Unitarian Universalism. I've
been Unitarian Universalist for forty-one years. I grew up
Unitarian Universalist. That was not a question for me
until I went into ministry. My colleagues were, without a
doubt, the hardest part of the transition into ministry.
One of the shocking experiences was colleagues explaining
Unitarian Universalism to me and it being incompatible
with the foundational Unitarian Universalism that I knew
in my bones. Just like I had to carve out my racial and
other identities from others who tried to stake a claim on
it. I had to carve out my faith from people who presume
they inherited Unitarian Universalism and want to
welcome me as a newcomer.

REV. MITRA RAHNEMA

———

Carolina, I make it a point to look at the little white wedding
Bible inscribed to her by John Haynes Holmes on her wedding
day. After Isaac and Gladys begat two sons, Glenn and Robert
McNatt, they raised them at Community Church in the 1960s
and 1970s. Thus I have my husband's dedication certificate signed
by Donald Harrington and his stories about Dick Leonard as his
Sunday school teacher in the sixth grade. All these things prepared him to introduce me to the faith I came to love and to
which I have dedicated my life; that is how our sons, Allen and
Daniel, are third-generation African-American Unitarian Universalists. As the only "come-inner" in the family, I am Unitarian
Universalist by temperament, not by birth. I have admittedly
overcompensated by becoming a UU minister, and I have been

around way too long to underestimate how problematic it can be to be a person of color in this faith.

Yet I feel possessive of this faith into which I married, for I hold in my mind's eye the Black matriarchs and patriarchs who first introduced me to *their* Unitarian Universalism forty years ago, who taught me how to do church, who first told me about Fannie Barrier Williams and Josephine St. Pierre Ruffin and Florida Ruffin Ridley—all Black women of an earlier era who also found themselves committed to our free but imperfect faith. Because of all these things, Unitarian Universalism is mine. I represent it as myself as best I can, in every arena that I can. In these days, I have embraced the responsibility of helping to train our next generation of ministers as president of Starr King School for the Ministry. As the first person of color to lead a UU seminary, and as one of a handful of women of color to lead a

———

We are planting the seeds. Maybe fifty years from now, there might be people who look up to you and me the way Rosemary looks up to her elders from forty years ago. I can't really wrap my head around that. But there aren't enough of us to be able to be mentors to the next generation. I went to Finding Our Way Home this past spring, and I was blown away! Who were all these young people who are coming up in our ranks as professionals of color? I'd never even seen most of them before. That was a gift and a blessing, just to see that. It was also odd feeling like I'm an elder compared to where many of them are at in their journey.

REV. MANISH MISHRA-MARZETTI

Where is the ancestral line, and what does it mean if we are seeding the ancestry of the next generation? I think about that as a woman and as a scholar. I have a mentor who didn't have a single Black professor during her program of study. As a member of the second generation in my field, I benefit from the women who have gone before me. What I ask them more than anything else is how the hell they survived when they were alone, because I can't imagine it. What do we offer our colleagues in terms of support? I heard so loud and clear that it's important for yourself and those around you to reconnect with the community, and to be in dialogue in those ways. What does that look like when you are carrying or birthing that potential yourself?

REV. SOFIA BETANCOURT

———

seminary in North America, I have a tremendous responsibility to my people and to my faith. It is a responsibility I am proud to assume. It is my way of serving the God who called me to this work, and who holds me still.

THE RELIGIOUS EDUCATOR OF COLOR

Rev. Natalie Maxwell Fenimore and
Aisha Hauser, MSW

ONE CHALLENGE FOR THE religious education professional of color is the tension between being a prophetic voice and maintaining a pastoral role for people of color in a mostly White denomination. The prophetic role is to build multiracial, multicultural, anti-oppressive Unitarian Universalism by teaching it, preaching it, and modeling it in our faith development programs and our faith development community culture. The pastoral role is to stand with individuals of color who are hurting, questioning, angry, and rejoicing about finding a Unitarian Universalism that is not yet the beloved community it seeks to become.

At the outset of their ministry to children, youth, and families, the religious educator is often particularly concerned with how to minister to White people as a person of color. While the minister of color, whose primary role is as a preacher, has to face the projections and perceptions of the White members of the congregation as well, the religious educator has the added layer of being in a ministry that encompasses the area of family making. Family making brings a particular intimacy into the relationship between religious professionals and congregants. To be called to be with people as they grow their souls and seek meaning over a lifetime is a gift—and a great responsibility. Issues of race, culture, and class complicate this journey in so many ways, for both the professional and those they try to serve.

There are some girls in our congregation who are now seniors in high school, and they just launched. They're biracial. There's this intimacy of knowing we have a lot in common, but how do we broach the subject? We've done a lot of things together. This is really a vulnerability on my part. We have a relationship and we love each other, but I feel like there's this huge missed opportunity, and I don't know what to do with that inherent intimacy that feels almost awkward.

REV. LAUREN SMITH

————

Religious educators and ministers and members of Unitarian Universalist congregations and communities have to push back against stereotypes of themselves and of others. The religious educator of color must contend with the images of servant, mammy, and caretaker, which have negative and derogatory connotations in American culture, while trying to do the good work of a helping profession. It can be necessary for the person of color to consider whether to be seen cleaning up after a congregational event or whether to cook for the holiday party. A White male minister may get credit for doing these things, but how will a Black woman be seen if she does these same domestic tasks? And will there be confusion and even anger if she refuses?

As with the dominant culture outside our congregations, UU congregations may not adequately honor the importance of working with children, youth, and families. The professional religious educator may be labeled, consciously or unconsciously, as doing traditional "women's work," which has for so long been unpaid and unheralded in the church, the home, and the wider community.

Unitarian Universalist communities and staff and ministry structures must strive to present images that can counter those so very present in society at large. That is what our religious education programs do in the ways that we develop curricula and set up learning experiences; for instance, we present multicultural images of families, including LGBT families, telling stories from many cultures, honoring many religious traditions. But this work is only partially successful if we do not counteract how religious education professionals are treated in UU communities. Is the work honored? Are duties, salaries, and benefits comparable?

When the religious educator of color is also the only, or one of the few, religious professionals of color in the congregation or other UU community, this dynamic is compounded. It is not unusual for the religious professional of color to be identified as the support staff or facilities staff and not as a professional staff member.

We have to be clear that when we invite people of color in, we're inviting them into a difficult place where the options available to them are both a gift and a curse.
They can do and be anything they want. What the religious educators of color and the ministers of color can provide is more information about the system. We can say, for instance, "Fine, don't connect your children of color to anybody else of color, but I can tell you how that's probably going to play out for you. If that is your choice, that is your choice, and this community will walk that walk with you and help you pick up the pieces, but there will be pieces that have to be picked up."

REV. NATALIE MAXWELL FENIMORE

In congregations with hierarchical governance models, the religious education lay professional is often not a part of the executive team. While this may appear to be an objective management decision, it can, in fact, amplify the perception that the religious education professional of color is not a decision-making leader. The religious educator can feel marginalized and disrespected—and unable to bring the issues of families of color to the leadership table.

A question we don't often ask ourselves but that is as important, if not more important, than the question of ministering to Whites, is this: How do I, as a person of color, minister to other people of color within Unitarian Universalism? What are my relationship and my obligation going to be to the spiritual health and faith formation of people of color within Unitarian Universalism?

This is a critical question for all ministers and religious professionals of color in Unitarian Universalism, but it is especially critical for the religious educator of color because the religious education community within our faith movement is the location of the most diversity. Our religious education programs and communities attract families longing for a place that welcomes and reflects the diversity that they may have in their own families—interracial, intercultural, multicultural families formed through birth or adoption—as well as families of color with young children developing racial identity within an overwhelmingly White religious community.

And so we find ourselves as religious educators, in what is often the most diverse population in our congregations, engaged in ministering to families of color who are trying to grow vital and healthy souls in what can look like an unwelcoming, noninclusive environment. The religious educator of color is often walking alongside people of color who are members of the congregation or in the youth group, or whom they meet at camps and conference centers and in online forums. We are orienting them to Unitarian Universalism and interpreting it, and providing

*If we have more variety in our professional ministries,
we give our families more information, more examples,
more resources, more people to walk different roads with
them. There are roads with them I can't walk. I can learn
about them. So that means that I do feel obligated to be
trained, to be aware of multiculturalism. I was able to
tell a parent about Korean Lunar New Year, something
she didn't know even though she was Korean American,
because she had dropped all that to assimilate. It's my
ability as a professional to give that as a gift back to her
family as an option, and that's what our ministries can
do. We can help people to be whole in some very serious
ways by giving them back their ability to claim parts
of themselves they had to drop along the way to be
successful Americans. So for me as a person of color,
that's something that perhaps comes to my awareness
differently than for a person of European descent.
So that's what I think that we can do, especially in
religious education, because people are at such a
vulnerable place. They're trying to figure out what their
faith can offer them for a lifetime going forward, and in
my role as a lifespan religious education professional,
I'm responsible for the people from the nursery
to the grave.*

REV. NATALIE MAXWELL FENIMORE

a space to explore the cultural and racial contexts of our faith tradition.

This is a mixed bag of experiences. While on the one hand, our faith professes solidarity with the oppressed and marginalized, Unitarian Universalism's demographics do not reflect the diversity of society at large. Religious educators of color find themselves invited to represent the welcome of diversity into Unitarian Universalism with their very bodies—their physical presence is the invitation to others. We carry the welcome. We embody the multicultural vision and the commitment of the faith to that vision.

————

I got a call a couple of weeks ago from another religious educator of color, and they said, "Well, the parents want to talk about race with the youth," and I said, "First you have to talk about it with the parents, because the parent is the primary religious educator. That's true. If we're lucky, we get them for four hours a week, maybe two hours."

AISHA HAUSER

————

We are often quickly invited into the personal life of the parent of a child of color in a Unitarian Universalist community. We can find ourselves in intimate and gut-wrenching decisions about child rearing—and in some funny moments too.

Parents of color might ask the religious educator of color to work with them to incorporate the history, theology, and traditions of their racial and cultural groups into the UU community. Families of color might ask, "Can I still honor Jesus? My parenting is more conservative than what I see here. Why is that? Why don't you dress up for church? Why don't you have a basketball court? How do you treat your elders? Why aren't the children in the worship service more? Help me—my young Black son was stopped by the police!"

People in multiracial or multicultural families have asked religious educators of color such questions as, "How do I comb her hair? Should I take her to Chinese school? My husband is from a Muslim family; will you teach anything about Islam?" There are so many stories. White parents have told religious educators that they feared they would never completely connect with their children of color. White parents have found themselves completely unprepared for the isolation their children of color experience at Unitarian Universalist camps and conference centers where they have no peers of color. White parents have confessed their discomfort with their children dating those from Muslim backgrounds. The religious educator of color sits and listens to these stories—sits with the pain of the parents and the children involved. It is not unusual for the same parents who did such deep sharing to then pull away because they are embarrassed and afraid of their own revelations. When parents move to push aside the relationship and not acknowledge professionalism in these interactions, it can be hard for the religious educator of color not to experience them as painful spiritual domestic work.

The professional may have to organize people of color groups or caucuses or small group ministry or reading groups. When they do this work, they have to be wary of becoming the focus of the confusion and even anger of some White members of the community who may be shocked at not having their interests at the center for the first time. Does supporting families of color put our jobs at risk? Maybe.

The professional religious educator is often the advocate for children, youth, and young adults of color—forging racial identity development and faith development. This work gives rise to a myriad of emotions for everyone—anger, confusion, sadness, frustration. The religious educator of color is often a bridge, stretched in all directions, trying to connect everyone through our faith. It can be exhausting.

For religious educators of color, there is also the role of "representing race" in Unitarian Universalism. People come in different shapes, sizes, and colors. On the face of it, there is no problem with that—it is an opportunity to celebrate the expansive genius of creation. However, human cultures put greater value on some sizes, shapes, and colors than others. Seeing a person of color as a religious professional in UU congregations is an announcement to the world that we are antiracist and multicultural. As a lay leader of a UU congregation said, "It would be great for our young people to see a person of color in the pulpit as an example." While people are often told that they can be themselves—individuals in UU community—the minister or religious educator of color is often denied that individuality and asked to represent race instead. This can be spiritually draining and sometimes insulting. It does not take into account the individuality of the person.

Ministers and religious educators of color are individuals. We have different and specific backgrounds. We cannot be all things to all people. One person cannot represent all the ways that Black, Latinx, Middle Eastern, Native American, Asian/Pacific Islander people—or anyone—move through Unitarian Universalism. For the religious professional of color not to be recognized as an individual is painful. For Unitarian Universalist congregations and communities to learn to relate to people of color in their uniqueness, while also acknowledging their historical cultural context, is both a learning opportunity and a spiritual exercise.

For religious professionals of color to do all that we must do as religious educators—to offer a prophetic and pastoral voice—we must have continuing professional development. The congregation, community, supervisor, and Unitarian Universalist Association must provide supportive learning experiences in workshops, classes, gatherings, and trainings. Time and financial support are essential. So much must be learned—information about different cultures and how-tos in multicultural learning, pastoral support, and identity development. The professional is challenged to move outside their comfort zone as much as any member of a congregation and community where they find themselves.

————

I'm constantly struggling with which response to choose. Early on in my ministerial development, I had a really difficult interaction with a powerful person in our denomination who was referring to me as Ayatollah. I wasn't exactly sure what to do. One mentor of color advised me to choose a pastoral response. That was smart advice as it is a brilliant ministerial tool to use. But I couldn't swallow it. Now I'm finding more and more in my ministry that I am less and less willing to engage with that kind of thing. There are people I actually refused to be with one-on-one anymore, which was a really difficult boundary to set because it erodes my sense that ministry "meets people where they are at." It is a constant tension in the context of racism— the need to decide which skill or tool to use in what situation and the criteria with which to make that decision.

REV. MITRA RAHNEMA

Self-care is a term that is used often and almost casually in Unitarian Universalist professional circles, but it is essential to the survival of the religious education professional of color. The ministry they provide in our communities is a ministry of presence, of accompaniment, of attentiveness. This ministry invites in the whole person. It is not easy; our buttons get pushed very, very often.

It is possible to swallow your feelings in order to get the job done, to assist others, or to see the emotions of others as being more important than your own. It is also the case that the dominant White culture and UU culture can view expressions of emotion by people of color as unprofessional, overwrought, or not intellectually valid. So where do you go for relief and support? Find a place or make a place. Be with colleagues of color; find a UU community of color separate from the place where you work.

Be clear with those in communities that you serve that you cannot be everything to everyone in the religious education community. Invite other professionals on staff to be present in the religious education community. White colleagues can be a resource for White families struggling with questions about race, class, and culture. White colleagues can teach and preach about issues of race, class, and culture. We must share the work in order to maintain our spiritual health.

While they can be diminished by the challenges of the role, the purpose and joy that exist for the Unitarian Universalist religious educator/minister of color make this a wonderful and fulfilling ministry.

RESPONSE TO NATALIE MAXWELL FENIMORE AND AISHA HAUSER

Rev. Sofia Betancourt

I WANT TO BEGIN BY thanking Aisha and Natalie, as well as the Committee for Antiracism and Multiculturalism (CARAOM), for ensuring that the gifts and needs of religious education professionals of color are well represented in this important gathering. Too often when considering the needs of religious professionals of color and of the settings in which we serve, the focus is solely on an ordained ministry. This is not only a profound disservice to our gifted colleagues but it also undermines the health and well-being of the very communities all of us work so hard to support.

Our writers Aisha and Natalie ask a frequently unexplored question about our obligation to the spiritual health and faith formation of people of color in the Unitarian Universalist community: "How do I, as a person of color, minister to other people of color within Unitarian Universalism? What is my relationship, my obligation going to be to the spiritual health and faith formation of people of color within Unitarian Universalism?" I had the privilege of serving for four years as the director for Racial and Ethnic Concerns for the Unitarian Universalist Association. This experience offered me various points of entry into communities and congregations across our movement that were developing an antiracist, anti-oppressive, multicultural ministry. Many times this work resulted in gatherings like this one, where a group of committed Unitarian Universalists would come together to identify best practices, share difficult truths, and refocus our work for

I was credentialed as a religious educator at the master's level before I was ordained, and I was so isolated because I was not on the ministerial track. I was serving a congregation where I was in charge of religious education programs for three hundred children. I trained and oriented and gathered more than a hundred volunteers in my congregation every year. I was the person who told them what Unitarian Universalism was about. None of you were there and none of you were part of mentoring me. None of you were part of knowing what I know, nor I part of knowing what you know. The people who mentored me when I came to Unitarian Universalism as a twenty-year-old were mostly White. A group of older White women scooped me up and took care of me as I learned my way in Unitarian Universalism, and that was sometimes problematic but full of love for me. It might have served me as a congregant. It was not a great model for ministerial formation for a person of color.

REV. NATALIE MAXWELL FENIMORE

———

the journey ahead. Over time I noticed several of our committed regulars giving feedback about the very obligation that Natalie and Aisha name. They pointed out the UUA's tendency to fund events where UUs who identify as people of color or as Latinx or Hispanic would learn about dismantling racism together. They wondered aloud when we might have the opportunity to organize some of our meetings around theological beliefs and spiritual practices for UUs of color. What would it mean if we did not have to justify our time together with an antiracist, anti-oppressive, multicultural agenda that many of us were already committed to, thanks to the good work of those who had organized before us?

When I was a student at Starr King School for the Ministry, I had the gift of participating in the early years of Rev. Lilia Cuervo's Spanish language ministry at First Unitarian Church of San Jose. Right away I noticed how centralized the needs and experiences of families were to the worship life of the community. I remember how Lilia often expressed the need to provide strong religious education as a first inroad into serving Latinx communities well. She recommended hiring a religious educator before a parish minister, something that would still be considered radical today. In essence, she reminded us of the primacy of faith formation for spiritual growth and wellness. I believe this is true across many communities of color, and I agree with Aisha and Natalie that a religious education professional of color provides a recognition of self and invitation into spiritual health that are badly needed among UUs of color.

What I hear emphasized time and again in their essay is how rarely the primary needs of UUs of color are fully considered in UU congregations. *Consideration* is key to this reflection. Students at Starr King tell me that worship works best for them

––––––

*I just grieve because I so look forward to getting together
in communities like this and not talking about white
people. I just don't want to talk about white people.
I grieve that we're still in a place in which it's really
important for us to talk about how we respond to racism,
how to exist in a system where that's part of our reality.*

REV. LAUREN SMITH

when they believe worship leaders have considered their presence in the room. This does not mean that every worship service has to speak directly to their needs or beliefs, but rather that someone has considered their presence and participation in the community and the impact of the congregation's celebration for them. This consideration can be reflected in something as simple as a one- or two-sentence acknowledgment that our backgrounds and socioeconomic locations mean we do not always believe or experience the same things, or in something as large and vital as doing

---

It's not that I can't sing. I won't sing. I chose to disrupt the ideal of who Black women are, so I don't sing. I made a conscious decision to emphasize the life of the mind. It disturbed people, made White people nervous, and that was a good thing in the sixties and seventies. I wonder what I paid for that. How do we manage the performance piece when we're not there to perform?

REV. ROSEMARY BRAY MCNATT

---

the hard work of reducing cultural misappropriation so that no one is made to feel their role in congregational life is to entertain others through their diversity.

This need for consideration can be applied to many painfully recognizable moments. Whether it is that a member never considered a person of color might be a wonderful fit for their congregation as a minister or director of religious education and is therefore shocked when one of us has the authority to do more than hold the door on a Sunday morning, or that a member never considered that children of color would participate in UU camps and conference centers and have needs specific to their identities, or that a member never considered that youth and young adults of color might lead us in work as vital as that of the Black Lives Matter movement, or that a member never considered that religious education might serve as the vital center of an authentic multicultural ministry and should not be stereotyped as a lesser offering in our congregations, the overarching lack of consideration diminishes our communities. The question is: Who do we *expect* ourselves to be?

Natalie and Aisha tell us that their words of assistance or advice or just being there while a White parent raises a child of color or while a parent of color raises a child of color in the largely White UU congregation is nothing less than a theological imperative—one that can exact a heavy toll. For that theological imperative to become an applied theology, we need tools that empower. There is no question in my mind that religious education professionals of color play a primary role in ministering to members and families of color as well as multiracial and multiethnic families and community members, in addition to all their other responsibilities. Part of the challenge, I imagine, is that *people of color* is a term we use as a political act to build coalitions to dismantle the effects of White supremacy on multiple oppressed or underserved racial and ethnic identities, and it does not, in fact, automatically make any of us an expert on communities outside our own. That ability to partner well with the families least likely to find their spiritual health and faith formation needs fully considered in our congregations requires professional training that religious leaders are not necessarily expected to have.

Congregations should already be prioritizing professional development expenses for their religious educators. In response to the sacred partnering with families so beautifully described by Aisha and Natalie, congregations should also particularly support them, whether or not they identify as people of color, in pursuing

The next generation of ministers should be required to learn about how to counter oppression. They should learn about intersectionality and about the ways in which different oppressions relate to and reinforce one another. I think it equips people to look at the world in which we live and actually understand and deconstruct some things that they experience in congregational life. There are people who want and need the skills we teach, and we need to find a way to help them get it. We should be strategizing about how to make sure ministers are equipped for the things they're going to face, both outside in the world and inside their congregations.

REV. ROSEMARY BRAY MCNATT

———

training in cross-cultural counseling, pedagogies, and faith formation needs. This is one way we might take the time to understand where families need support. Another possibility is connecting with the work of organizations like the MAVIN Foundation, which specifically explores the gifts and blessings of raising children in multiracial families.

Unitarian Universalism will never succeed in building beloved community while refusing to consider religious professionals of color as anything more than a confirmation of our own goodness. The moment of hire is not our pinnacle of success. It is a moment of possibility. Here, together, we might partner in reimagining the spiritual journey that is to come. Here, in community, we are blessed with partners who might build alongside us a Unitarian Universalism for the twenty-first century. The question that remains is who do we expect ourselves to become?

HOW DARE YOU? *MI LIKKLE, BUT MI TALLAWAH!*

Rev. Dr. Hope Johnson

T HE PHONE RANG. It was Leslie Takahashi, chair of the UUMA Nominating Committee, asking, "Hope, would you be willing to serve as Continental Good Offices Person?" It would mean serving on the UUMA board for two consecutive terms, since I was at the time completing my term as the ARAOM (Anti-Racism, Anti-Oppression, and Multicultural Ministries) portfolio holder. Could I do it? Would I be willing to do that?

Is the sky blue? "Would I be willing?" You bet! I was ready. I had been primed. I knew that I could do it. My dream for service to the Unitarian Universalist Ministers Association had come true. *Yes!*

And then, a few hours later, my phone rang.

I received a phone call that would turn my UU life as a leader upside down, a phone call from someone I had looked up to, a respected leader in Unitarian Universalism; someone whom I had considered to be a dear friend, a loyal friend; someone who had visited me in New York and stayed at my home; someone whose family I had come to know and love. This was the person who had taught me everything I know about collegiality: Pick up the phone, the e-mail, the text. Say yes when called and figure out *how* later.

So I get this call. It is my friend at the other end of the line.

"Hi."

"Hi, Hope."

"How goes?" We exchanged pleasantries. I know that he's calling to congratulate me on being nominated to serve as Continental Good Offices Person. *Yes!*

"Hope, I'm calling to support you."

"Okay," I responded, while dancing a happy dance.

"Hope, you should not take on the role of Good Offices Person. You'll be in way over your head. I can help you to get out of it."

"*What?*"

Now I'm steaming. "Get out of my dream volunteer position for the UUMA? Are you kidding?"

It went farther south from there.

In my mind I'm screaming, *Who on earth do you think you are? How dare you call me with this no-confidence vote? Who or what gives you the authority and temerity to tell me you are calling to "support" me?*

In Jamaica, where I am from, we often say that we are, as a nation "*likkle but tallawah.*" Loosely translated, it means that though we are a tiny country, in many ways we are a mighty people with a huge presence and a profound impact on the world. This phrase came back to me at this moment. Thank God that I had something non-UU to fall back on, something that reminded me I could let go of worrying, because "every little thing's gonna be alright," as Bob Marley sang. Though I tried to ease the tension in my head, I didn't know what to do with my heart, which had been broken into pieces too numerous to pick up.

My learned and earned culture of politeness and deference didn't allow me to say all that I was thinking and feeling. All I could do was to muster up a "thanks, but no thanks" before hanging up.

I was livid! I was hurt. I was bewildered and couldn't believe what I had just experienced. In that one phone call, my faith in Unitarian Universalism just about died. Soon after that, my faith in myself began to dissipate.

When I was a young girl I had given up on organized religion. There I was in Sunday school, so tired of getting into trouble each and every Sunday that God made. Why? Because I was asking too many questions about God, Jesus, Mary, Adam and Eve, and the virgin birth. I was in trouble for not taking a story at face value, for disbelieving. I never understood the significance of the Trinity and couldn't understand why I couldn't have a direct line to my friend God. "Because it simply is" and "because it's in the Bible" were simply not adequate responses, at least not for me.

Thankfully, my dad understood and gave me permission to quit Sunday school. We agreed to religious instruction about different faiths at home each week and attending a house of worship at least every other week. I was free to choose a church, synagogue, mosque, temple, or any other house of worship wherever we were living. I loved experiencing the diversity of worship and always entered a new faith community with an open heart in my effort to continue my relationship with God. Knowing that I was right with God was enough for me, so I chose not to join anything.

Eventually, I ended up at the Community Church of New York, a Unitarian Universalist congregation in midtown Manhattan that had a diverse membership. One group that Community welcomed was the West Indian Students Association, under the leadership of its president, my dad, Keith Johnson. This was a group that John Haynes Holmes hosted back in the day in the mid-1990s. I recall walking into the informal worship space of what would become my home church on a hot Sunday morning in August. I was immediately struck by the array of banners that represented many of the world's religions and made me feel theologically at home. I enjoyed the service—the music, the sermon, the ambiance.

But I also recall that after service was over, I did not enjoy the rush to welcome me as folks asked, "Where are you from?" "What brought *you* here?" "How did you hear about Community Church?" "How *on earth* did you hear about Unitarian Universalism?" The usual questions that felt—and still feel—awkward

Unitarian Universalism is who I am. It's in my bones.
How else, where else, can I do and be what I'm doing
and being? I have, at one point in time or another,
thought about every other possible thing I could do
with my life. I've thought about leaving parish
ministry. I've thought about going into military
chaplaincy, going into hospital chaplaincy, going into
teaching. I've thought about doing this as a Hindu
spiritual leader. I've thought about doing this as a
UCC minister. I've thought about doing this as a
Unity Church minister. I literally have thought about
and actively played out in my mind each of these
scenarios, and they just don't make sense to me. The
path I am on is the path that makes sense to me. I
realize that Unitarian Universalism will never in my
lifetime be what I would like it to be, and maybe even
in my bones need it to be, and yet this is the context in
which I can be most free to be who I am. So both of
these things are true at the same time, and that is
really hard. Obviously if you enter ministry you're
idealistic. And if you're idealistic, you want things to
line up in ways that make sense, that are logical and
in perfect congruence. And that doesn't exist for me.
It doesn't exist for many of us.

REV. MANISH MISHRA-MARZETTI

to me as I was reminded, even as I was welcomed, that I was the other.

I tried to sneak out of Community just as fast as I possibly could, without drawing any attention to myself. Uh-oh! "Hope? Janice Marie? I'd recognize you anywhere. Welcome!" A warm welcome from an old family friend—actually, my godmother's best friend. She not only asked about everyone, as I squirmed, but then proceeded to introduce shy-me-who-was-just-trying-to-get-out-of-there-Hope to *everyone*. Sigh.

"See you next week. . . ."

And wouldn't you know, I went back every single Sunday after that. I had found my faith home—though I had not been looking for one.

Unitarian Universalism scooped me up, and I in return tightly embraced my beloved faith, quickly claiming it as my own. I knew I had joined something that was a frame for me—for my beliefs, my values, my aspirations, for all that I lived and worked for.

Community Church of New York had high expectations of me—not only as member but also as leader. I didn't seek to become a leader, but within a short period of time there I was—a front-runner! I continued to study Unitarian Universalism long after the classes for new UUs were over. I was determined to understand the workings of this faith.

Opportunities for leadership development were often offered, including financial and logistical support for first timers headed to General Assembly. I actually thought that was "the UU way" and only learned years later that what I had experienced was not representative of all UU congregations. In fact, I would eventually discover that many of the leaders did not see themselves as such. And many others who were offered the same opportunities that I had did not recognize them as invitations for integration into membership or leadership development.

My first year in seminary, a minister of color pushed me up against the wall and told me that Starr King and the UUA were not to be trusted and all that they would do to me as a minister of color. All his rage was literally pressing my body against the wall. This is my first memory of issues of race in Unitarian Universalist ministry, and that was from a minister of color whom we had harmed. So I live with that fear when I do my best to mentor as many folks as I can, because there are not enough of us ministers of color. I'm supposedly an elder because we've lost so many of our elders that there is a vacuum. There is no way that, in fourteen years, I should be an elder. That is a sign of ill health in our denomination. I am triple guessing myself as a mentor, because I'm torn between repeating what the system has put into me and saying, "Here are the twelve stories I don't think you know yet because no one has told you." We have a silencing culture, but I don't know how we can tell a new story until our culture changes around how we find our way through call. We need to be better clearance committees for each other. We need to even understand better how clearance committees work and create a structure of strength. I don't think any of us would be in this room if we weren't in love and committed in some way, even if it's to a Unitarian Universalism we may never see.

REV. SOFIA BETANCOURT

I dived into congregational life head-first and quickly became interested in almost every aspect of it. Truth be told, I had arrived at what would become my home congregation somewhat sure of who I was in my world. Within a relatively short period I had taken on leadership in the congregation. I knew my way around this community, my spiritual neighborhood. I lived, to the best of my ability, the language of Unitarian Universalism. Before too long, I was engaged in leadership on the district and then the associational level. I had become a religious leader.

It was, without question, as a lay leader that I answered the call to professional ministry. As a professional minister I chose to always honor not only professional ministry but also the gift that shared ministry brings. I promised myself I would always remember to present my *authentic* self to relationships. I innocently asked, "What's not to love?" and decided that I would *never* give up the essence of Hope. Little did I know how difficult that would be.

I moved through Unitarian Universalism, first as a layperson and then as a minister, with a strong sense of ownership. The expectations that I would be an asset to this religion were high. Investments were placed in my potential as a leader and as a bridge builder. Because of that, I have fully embraced Unitarian Universalism. Wherever I went, I was welcomed as a leader.

My colleagues often speak of the phenomenon of the "golden child," but I usually think about it more in terms of shiny, newly minted "platinum" leaders. The phenomenon is often evident at General Assembly: the leader who is suddenly *everywhere*, on stage, on panels. The UUA has a tendency to lift up one leader at a time. Unfortunately, it too often feels like the ice cream flavor of the month, and it happens all too often in Unitarian Universalism, particularly for persons from historically marginalized groups. This is a lesson that most of us from the margins end up learning through unexpectedly difficult experiences that we encounter and then have to navigate. There are no scripts for that.

How do we hold on to our own self-worth when we often
don't know whether we are being raised up because of who
we are and what skills we have or because we are people of
color? How do we find strength within that? I think in
particular about the people whom we have lost because they
got crushed by being raised up and then tossed to the side,
and they have not come back. How do we create support so
that when someone does become the flavor of the month,
we are there to catch them when they are tossed aside?

REV. DARRICK JACKSON

———

Service led me to the Unitarian Universalist Ministers Association (UUMA), where I served on ARAOM, first as a member and later as chair. From there I served on the Board of the UUMA as the portfolio holder for ARAOM. During one introduction, I described myself as the "sister from another planet," and everyone laughed. By then I knew that I didn't quite fit in. I was other. Yes, I was a leader who had worked hard, so hard. Yes, I had earned my stripes. But I recognized that though I was welcomed into the UUMA Board, I wasn't seen as someone who truly belonged. By then it was clear to me that I was not one of the representatives of the living legacy of authentic Unitarian Universalist ministry. There was an insider-outsider reality. And yet with time, I felt more and more comfortable at that Board table. In fact, I grew comfortable enough in my own authenticity to know deep in my heart and soul that I was holding the wrong portfolio. *Why should I hold the ARAOM portfolio just because I am a Person of Color?* I often asked myself. Sure, I could do the job, but that was not where my heart was. That was not where I felt I could effect the change I demanded of Unitarian Universalism, my chosen faith. I wanted the UUMA Board to adopt an anti-racist, anti-oppressive lens that celebrated multiculturalism in every endeavor. And I believed the time had come for people from the dominant culture to do this work—not me. My gifts and talents, my passion, related more directly to supporting my colleagues when their ministries were falling apart. My strength was in finding ways to support our ministry, our code of ethics. My strength was in keeping people at the table through the difficult moments of transition. Good Offices became a ministry, not a portfolio, and I knew that my calling at that time was to the ministry of Good Offices, not to ARAOM.

The time had come for a leader from the dominant culture to emerge—one who could, and would, successfully hold the ARAOM portfolio. We had a great committee that did meaningful work. We came up with a game plan that included making a way for the portfolio holder (me) to move from what I

———

If you want a certain position, a bigger footprint, then instead of doing what others think a person of color should do, go ahead and leave that bigger footprint and model that achievement for other people. There is the need to develop support systems for people who are out there trying to do the new thing and be on the edge. We should feel in relationship with other UU professionals of color so that when we see what they are trying to accomplish, we move toward them and assist in developing support systems that can make their accomplishments possible.

REV. NATALIE MAXWELL FENIMORE

experienced as the Black/White paradigm to a full embrace of multiculturalism. The first step was appointing Parisa Parsa, a well-respected minister who bridged many divides, to chair the Committee after I moved onto the Board. We then brought Josh Pawelek, an antiracist activist and strategist, on board. He replaced Parisa as Committee chair. Parisa joined the Board.

But there was a caveat: There had to be someone on the UUMA Board *at all times* who represented the other. That was a sea change for the Board.

By then there was no turning back. I felt compelled to do something new as a leader, and I knew that the place where my passion met my gifts and talents was Good Offices. I had sat at the feet of Fred Muir. I observed the care and attention that he placed in this ministry. I had served as a Good Offices Person at the chapter level, and I was struck by how often, during times of crisis, no thought was given to ARAOM concerns, even when it was obvious to me that this was an elephant in the room that should receive serious consideration.

All of my long evolution as a Unitarian Universalist was in the background when I received the phone call from Leslie asking me to serve as Continental Good Offices Person, and then the phone call from my colleague advising me to withdraw my candidacy. I had paid my dues. I had earned my stripes. I had knocked myself out. For what? To be reminded, once again, that I was the "sister from another planet." Good enough for good times. Good enough to host you at my home. Good enough to sit at the table holding the portfolio for persons of color to make Unitarian Universalism look good—but not good enough for the solid, meaningful ministry and work of Good Offices.

I was also insulted on behalf of my colleague Leslie. How could one of our trusted ARAOM allies undermine the work of the UUMA Nominating Committee chaired by our colleague *of Color?*

I've noticed patterns among some newer religious professionals of color: They want and seek out the high power, high profile White colleagues to be their mentors, and I have wondered about that. I have wanted at times to go up to these younger colleagues and say, "You really need a mentor of color—the wisdom and mentoring of those who have gone before you. You might not know or appreciate that. You might not see that right now, but I'm telling you, you need this." The newer colleague may be thinking, "Well, this White minister, with clout and recognition, is going to be a reference for me and promote my career ten or twenty years from now." Personally, I didn't pursue those kinds of training settings. I wonder sometimes if I made a mistake in not doing that. But then again, I have watched, over the past decade or so, colleagues of color who have pursued and secured high profile training settings struggle in the job search process anyway. They are not necessarily doing any better in search than any of the rest of us.

REV. MANISH MISHRA-MARZETTI

———

Never as a Unitarian Universalist minister have I been as hurt or as angry as I was when I received that call from a "well-intentioned" colleague. My heart was broken. Suffice it to say that I called Leslie. I had begun to doubt my self-worth and needed to be assured that I had been invited to serve *based 100 percent on merit*. I checked in with other respected leaders and asked them if they had any reservations about my ability to perform—with excellence—the duties of a Good Offices Person. I shared my concerns with family. I looked within my own heart. I prayed, and I knew that I would make a kick-ass Continental Good Offices Person. I knew that I had the gifts of listening, loving, communicating. I knew I could do it. And so I called Leslie *again* and said, "Count me in. I would *love* to serve as the UUMA's Continental Good Offices Person."

And I did. Was I perfect? No, but who is? I know that I served with distinction. I cared. I delivered. As a result of my leadership, the ministry of Good Offices has started to change to better reflect the times and meet today's needs. I am proud of my service.

But that didn't solve the problem of the broken relationship I now had with my colleague. Our children were close friends. My esteemed colleague had been one of my fiercest allies in the world of antiracism and anti-oppression, although he wished sometimes that I would be "angrier." I know myself. I was often angry, but when I am angry I simmer, I don't shout. I am not that stereotypical angry Black woman. I have a forgiving heart, but how on earth would I cross the bridge that would lead to restoration? Eventually, the question shifted from "How could I cross the bridge to him?" to "How could we both meet on that bridge?"

My call to covenant as a Unitarian Universalist is with me, even when I don't want to be reminded of it. When the focus shifted from my crossing the bridge to him to each of us crossing the bridge to the other, I was reminded of that wonderful Rumi quote: "Out beyond the ideas of wrongdoing and rightdoing there is a field. I'll meet you there."

I recall that we attended a meeting in San Antonio, Texas. We planned to have dinner together. I was uneasy, a nervous wreck. How could we eat together when we couldn't even speak together?

But I was game.

Why? Because right relationship meant, and means, everything to me. I simply could not stand not being in right relationship with this colleague. I recall teasing him on several occasions, telling him that I loved him—in spite of himself.

Well, the hour of reckoning had come.

———

I want to lean into the question of forgiveness and the shame that has come up around making difficult choices. There's this line in a Paul Simon song that says, "Believing I had supernatural powers, I slammed into a brick wall." I carry that line with me in ministry in these questions about taking up the mantle to transform our faith, questions about when we step into that, when we step out of that, and how much those issues of shame and forgiveness enter into it.

REV. LAUREN SMITH

———

"Take a chance, Hope," I said to myself, "one more chance. You'll feel better. You have *nothing to lose*. Have dinner and try to fix it."

I recall that I had a sip of white wine but could not eat. I had no appetite. But we talked. And we talked. And we talked. And I am clear that each of us wanted to be in right relationship with each other.

We agreed to disagree. He had really tried to protect me, because he feared that I would have been eaten up. Thankfully, I had had enough faith in myself as a Unitarian Universalist leader to know that his fears were totally misguided. I knew I could handle that portfolio.

I tell this story, with the permission of my friend, not to dwell on old conflict but because it speaks to the power of relationship—right relationship, the importance of honoring the inherent worth and dignity of each person.

This story reminds me of the incredible power of love.

It begins with wanting to make it right.

I keep looking for a mentor, and I've been here for twenty-five years now. I still need a mentor. It doesn't change just because I spent seventeen years in the ministry. I'm still looking for people to help me negotiate, figure out, deconstruct. It's what I'm challenged with constantly.

REV. DR. KRISTEN HARPER

Years later we revisited this painful time in our relationship. We considered the difference between impact and intent. He meant me no harm, yet he stands by his assertion that he was doing what he thought was best for Unitarian Universalism, for the Unitarian Universalist Ministers Association, and for me. I simply cannot understand where he is in all this. This has caused me to take a keen look at good intentions. I believe that his thinking and reasoning on this matter were, and are, wrong. True support would have looked different. It would have meant helping me to succeed as I fulfilled my ministry, not trying to stop me from taking it on. True support means being there through thick and thin and being there for me when I fail, as we all do sometimes. True support means being willing to believe in someone's potential even when it doesn't fit into your framework or context. I served well, so well that we can now agree to disagree—in love.

This was the most painful experience that I've had as a Unitarian Universalist, partly because it was so personal. Yet it has afforded me lessons that I would not otherwise have had.

The insidiousness of sexism, racism, and other prejudices got a lot clearer after this experience. Old patterns cannot easily be broken. We all have to keep working on our cross-cultural competency and engagement. My understanding of the workings of Unitarian Universalism has shifted so that now I better understand the power of the old boys and old girls networks. I accept the fact that I will never quite fit in, so I've embraced my identity and I continue to be that "sister from another planet."

───────

Often when we gather like this, as people of color in Unitarian Universalism, some acknowledgment of the good old girl or good old boy network occurs with regularity. We know that it is powerful in Unitarian Universalism. I want to encourage us to do more than name its existence, because we can't work on something that we're in denial about. You can work on something only when you turn in toward it, when you face it. I'm sure I'm not the only person who can attest to this: That network has little interest in supporting, cultivating, and furthering the careers of religious professionals of color. That is not the agenda of the leaders who are in those types of positions, who are accorded power, back channels of power, and influence. This reality is a real contributor to glass ceilings in our movement.

REV. MANISH MISHRA-MARZETTI

As I engage in ministry, I must embrace the everyday difficulties that I face. I must expect the curveballs hurled my way, the unexpected reminders that I am, indeed, other.

But I hold on to something greater. Unitarian Universalism has given me a legacy to continue living into. I'm one of the lucky ones in whom my congregation invested, and I have been blessed by Unitarian Universalism's investment in me. Over the years I feel I have become a "sister of *this* planet." So what exactly does that mean? In many ways I see myself as a mirror of Unitarian Universalism. Our religion is itself a "sister from another planet." It doesn't quite fit into the usual denominational or parish scene. It isn't a "typical" congregation, church, fellowship, temple, or mosque. It is other. And yet, the living tradition from which Unitarianism, Universalism, and Unitarian Universalism springs also and reminds us that Unitarian Universalism is the "sister of this planet."

———

It's a different conversation when you have some institutional power. I'd be curious if people might want to reflect on the idea of embracing instead of rejecting the position of being other or marginalized, otherized in some way—similar to the ethic of embracing queerness.

REV. MITRA RAHNEMA

———

This experience has made me a better colleague, mentor, and friend, a better religious leader. I'm more aware of power dynamics—not because I want to know *my* place but because I want to understand everyone's place in the system.

There's this way in which Unitarian Universalism is like someone who is actively navigating an addiction: You can be in love with them and hope for them and refuse to take responsibility for their addiction. I remember a quote about the sign over the gates of hell that says, "Abandon hope all ye who enter here," and how there's something beautiful about abandoning hope and making peace with what is; it allows for a fresher way of committing to the health and well-being of somebody. Those two things go together in a really lovely way. Giving up the hope that something can be better helps us to be in healthy relationship that has the capacity to be supportive. It's like with my kids: If I rescue them, they often don't do the thing that they can do or know they can do.

REV. LAUREN SMITH

Margaret J. Wheatley, author of the book *Turning to One Another*, reminds us:

In this turbulent time we crave connection; we long for peace; we want the means to walk through the chaos intact. . . . We cannot find connection, community, and peace by withdrawing from others or going unconscious. The peace we seek is found in experiencing ourselves as part of something bigger and wiser than our little, crazed self. The community we belong to is all of life. The turbulence cannot be controlled, but when we stop struggling and accept it as part of life, it feels different.

Unitarian Universalism can be a stellar leader in our world with aspirations for multicultural community. Though we still have to work real hard at it, the goal is for each member to not only be valued but also feel at home. The goal is for each of us to be encouraged to have a sense of ownership. Our renewed understanding of inclusion suggests that we no longer need a notion of other. Unitarian Universalism is moving from the language of otherness to the language of inclusion. I want to be a part of this!

Unitarian Universalism is in the unique position of being able to help us all remember our worth and dignity regardless of how difficult it is. This includes leaders. This includes me.

Response to Hope Johnson
Rev. Leslie Takahashi

W HEN HOPE CALLS and tells me what has happened, I am saddened. And I am reminded of a conversation I had, also within the Unitarian Universalist Ministers' Association (UUMA), in which a White female colleague pointed at me, a new appointee to the Nominating Committee and said, "I am tired of people rising above their competency just because they are people of color." I remember how, in that moment, only a couple years before this phone call with Hope, I too had been plunged into self-doubt. In that moment of accusation, I wondered why I *had* been offered a leadership position—and the fifteen-plus years of UU volunteerism and twenty-plus years of professional leadership, including work for three statewide organizations, one of them a leadership organization, vanished. In that moment, another colleague jumped in to change the subject and end the awkward silence. I tried to recall my resume while the accusing finger-pointer screwed up her face in disgust and did not meet my eyes again for the rest of the lunch.

Leading as a person of color in our Association—well, it *is* complicated. One walks between the world of one's experience and the world of the dominant culture, forever holding multiple truths. One sees the world through a lens that members of the dominant culture cannot perceive and finds it impossible to explain what it feels like on the other end of the accusing finger or the dismissive intervention.

I am on the phone with Hope, and I am pacing in my bathroom, which is where I go in my small house when there is a pastoral or other ministerial matter I do not wish my son to overhear.

I do not want him to overhear this—not about the faith I still hope he will want to inherit someday. I am hearing Hope's story, and it connects with so many I have heard over the years.

We set our leaders of color up to fail. We spin them into the stratosphere of incompetence by asking them to take on too many things. We hold them to different standards and then take them apart for not meeting the ones that they did not know existed. We dangle plum responsibilities before them that require large amounts of energy and time and then mutter about how they don't meet deadlines or responsibilities. Janice Marie Johnson, Hope's intrepid sister, once described this as the "people of color elevator to hell." One rises up very fast and then, just as fast, crashes to the ground. Death by opportunity.

Hope was not on this trajectory. She had served well and faithfully in a number of visible positions where she had demonstrated quiet competence, and yet here she was reeling, doubting herself—as stunned as I had been in that UUMA orientation lunch two years before. As she tells me what happened, I remember an African-American friend who served on the UUA Board for eight years and, in his seventh year, offered an opinion about the budget. A fellow Board member retorted with words to this effect: "Oh, you have an opinion about something not about race!"

These kinds of comments and actions have an inadequate word: *microaggressions*. This is an imperfect word because the *micro* part implies these aggressions are not damaging in a large way. The huge truth is they are.

The new forms of discrimination are more subtle than the kind experienced by Lewis McGee, Joseph Fletcher Jordan, and the other Black pioneers in our predominantly White religion, who were told they were not able to offer their gifts at our religious leadership table. Or by women such as Olympia Brown, who were told they could study for the ministry but were unlikely to get pulpits. The new forms are in some ways more painful.

*I have a senior White colleague who enthusiastically
volunteered to support me in the search process, and
then I later found out that this individual actively
supported another candidate for that same job. I was so
heartbroken and devastated, and in some ways, I still
am. Politics is part of most professional fields. I'm not
blind to this. But we are in the business of spirituality.
I grew very angry for some time. Ultimately, through
working with spiritual teachers and my own reflection
process, I saw that all I could do is either carry that
disappointment and anger for the rest of my life or find a
way to hand it back to the person who caused it. I asked
the concerned individual to talk with me. And what
happened next was maybe bold, maybe "un-Asian" of
me, because I handed it all back. I let this person know
how much hurt and pain they had caused me. As the
conversation unfolded, they were taken aback at the
impact they had had on me. I forgave them, but I almost
wonder if I was too quick in forgiving, perhaps because
this person was so clearly uncomfortable and remorseful.
I don't know what the right answer is. There's no "right"
answer to these types of situations. All we can do is try to
be our best selves in the moment, even when we're
blindsided, even when we feel betrayed.*

REV. MANISH MISHRA-MARZETTI

One article I return to again and again is Valerie Batts's "Is Reconciliation Possible?" She writes of what she calls "modern racism," which she contrasts with "old-fashioned racism." Her article is the perfect antidote for the conversation I have a couple times a year when some White Unitarian Universalist says, "Well, I was active before the sixties. We changed the laws. It's not like it was then. People aren't being lynched."

Laws, Valerie Batts points out, are easier to change than attitudes. As one of the Black children picked to integrate the schools after *Brown v. Board of Education*, she knows. Batts has worked to help people understand that blaming the victim, dysfunctionally rescuing people, and denying difference and its political significance are some of the more contemporary forms in which people preserve the underlying attitudes that are so corrosive.

I write this in the heartbreaking summer of 2016, when we don't need to be reminded that racial hatred is alive and well in the nation and the smoldering embers of hatred have become a roaring bonfire. The United States has much-touted laws against discrimination, but a law cannot force a person to step across their implicit and implanted fears of the other and try to understand someone who is different from them. Economic frustration and an increasingly polarizing media climate have amplified distrust and resentment. Americans of color have suffered tragic losses. Many Americans still fail to note the way a private prison industry and actual reversal of some of the lauded laws have created an insidious new institutional racism.

Hope's colleague was rescuing her from something from which she did not need to be rescued. He was also denying that in 2014 the role of Good Offices needed to be significantly different than it had been a decade before. Good Officers should be putting a high priority on helping religious professionals of color who find themselves ensnared in modern racial discord. Yet that system, because it denies that a minister of color—or a woman, for that matter—might have a different experience than a heterosexual White man, fails to serve more and more of our colleagues. By denying the political significance of difference, my good colleague who questioned Hope as the candidate did not understand that while she might not have brought the same sense of authority as some who preceded her in that office, she brought special gifts and intelligences that were just as needed.

Let us be clear. Modern racism wounds, and in the summer of 2016, we know it kills, because it keeps attitudes from changing and hatred from being healed with the balms of love. Microaggressions are like death by a thousand paper cuts. In that moment, Hope had to be reminded of all those small assaults. The impact was real, even with a colleague she considered a friend, someone who would never intentionally harm her.

A disturbing pattern of old-fashioned racism is increasingly evident. The very lives of black- and brown-skinned people are being targeted. Modern racism still exists and harbors hate the way the tiny bodies of mosquitoes hold deadly diseases.

Neither the finger-pointing colleague from my first UUMA leadership lunch nor the colleague who tried to discourage Hope (also someone I revere) could understand that our leaders of color may move more quickly into leadership not just because tokenism is still alive and well but also because they may have an

———

We are who we are all the time. We give ourselves as a gift. I don't see myself as a marginal person. I don't lead from the margins. My blackness and woman-ness are at the center of my being. I don't need anybody's permission to claim myself.

REV. NATALIE MAXWELL FENIMORE

intelligence needed in a UUA struggling mightily to keep up with a world that is already multicultural and complicated. These leaders of color know to their very bones and UU soul that in this new world, one needs to value all forms of knowing and the emotional intelligence that leaders of color get through the constant need to read multiple truths is a valuable tool in these paradoxical times.

I am still on the phone with Hope, and now my pacing has slowed because I know that she is in fact a leader and she does know what she brings, and while she is injured, she will carry on as so many of us in the small and yet growing community of color do each day. We do it because of our great and sustaining love for our faith, which calls on us to help make its promise real for all. Hope, my colleague, will carry on, and we all will learn a little about the implicit biases we don't even know we have and the skills we need to minister in this hurting world.

Faithful Stubbornness
Rev. Peter Morales

FOURTEEN YEARS AGO, expressing a frustration that had been growing for years, I told an audience of fellow ministers at the annual Ministry Days prior to General Assembly, "The UUA isn't racist; the UUA is *clueless*." I was critical of the language and concepts we were using in our antiracism, anti-oppression, multi-culturalism efforts. (I remember irreverently calling it "anti-anti-M.") The thrust of my criticism was that our language was too concentrated on race and that we were ignoring the importance of both social class and culture. In addition, I believed that our focus on Black-White tensions ignored major groups like Latinxs, Asians, and Native Americans—not to mention the tens of millions of people, mostly young people, whose racial and

---

The African–American experience is the normative narrative of the marginalized in Unitarian Universalism (and in the wider American culture). That narrative, powerful in my own life, makes it more, not less, difficult to know about experiences lived out of different cultural realities. As we navigate the complexities of identity, it is less analysis and more grace that we require. And grace is a place in our tradition where we have always needed more work.

REV. DR. WILLIAM SINKFORD

ethnic mixture simply doesn't fit any of these categories. Our categories described an America that no longer existed. The Unitarian Universalist Association has come a long way since then. Today we are far more nuanced in our understanding.

Of course, race continues to matter in America. One unfortunate and unintended consequence of our using the term *people of color* is that it draws attention away from the particularly pernicious oppression suffered by poor African Americans. The steady stream of news about Black men being killed with impunity by law enforcement and incidents of racially motivated violence are chilling reminders that Black people face oppression that is systemic and violent.

And it is also true that a combination of intermarriage and immigration continues to complicate any discussion of racism and oppression. Hispanics have been the largest minority group for some time. The oppression they suffer is different in many ways. Just as importantly, increased intermarriage and interracial adoption defy the neat categories that made sense a generation or two ago. What category do we apply to a child who is half Korean and half Mexican American or to someone who has an Anglo father and a Chinese mother? At the most personal level, what do we call my children, who have a Latinx (Mexican American and Spanish ancestry) father and a bilingual Anglo (English and Irish ancestry) mother? What are they to call themselves? And what about my new grandson? It gets complicated.

The Visible: The First Latinx to Be X, Y, and Z

One challenge any of us ministers of color face in navigating our roles is that, while the larger world around us is changing rapidly, so is Unitarian Universalism. Let me illustrate this with a bit of my own story. My own journey as a UU has been dizzying and instructive.

I want to talk about the journey with the term people of color. *I actually don't know anyone who uses that term to describe their personal identity rather than understanding their family dynamic, the history of their cultures, their best writers. It's a label one picks up as an act of solidarity and coalition building. But Leon Spencer, who has mentored so many of us, would say to us, "Who benefits from what was just said? How is the system working to reestablish itself through what was just said, and how are we being encouraged to fight for the breadcrumbs thrown off the table so that the table can dine in peace?"* People of color *is the term used to prevent us from fighting over the nickel that fell off the $10-million budget. My journey with that term is as a Unitarian Universalist of color, as a proud Latina, as a proud woman of African descent, as a multiracial, multiethnic woman who does not feel that she is built up of parts. Rita Nakashima Brock speaks about interstitial integrity, the wholeness of the in-between. All of what we talk about is about returning to our community, so I may choose the term* people of color *because it means that I am aligning my work, my spirit, and my unpaid efforts with my community rather than with an institution that believes it's my job to drag it along behind me. Our own accountability to community organizing, I hope, can be a primary commitment in how we move forward.*

REV. SOFIA BETANCOURT

In 1996, a few weeks shy of my fiftieth birthday, I entered seminary. I was relatively new to Unitarian Universalism, though I was one of those who had been UU without knowing it for decades. As I drove the rental truck down Interstate 5 from Oregon to Berkeley to attend Starr King School for the Ministry, I had no idea that I would soon find myself in the midst of our movement's particular struggles around race. I didn't know the history, but I was soon helping to write the next chapter.

I had heard about the Spanish-language outreach ministry in San Jose, California. A fellow seminarian and I went down to check it out, and I soon found myself involved. The first sermon I gave in my life was delivered in my somewhat rusty Spanish to eight people. I was terrified. My sermon, "Cruzando Fronteras," spoke of crossing both personal and political frontiers. (The title means "Crossing Borders" or "Crossing Frontiers." *Frontera* is used to mean both a national border and a frontier and makes for a nice play on words.)

More invitations soon followed. I was invited to spend a week in Boston in January at Extension Ministry training, and then to attend a gathering of ministers and seminarians of color. That meeting had about forty or fifty attendees, including such notables as Bill Sinkford, Marjorie Bowens-Wheatley, Mel Hoover, Jacqui James, Abhi Janamanchi, Patricia Jimenez, and Jose Ballester. It led to the formation of the group that was later to become Diverse Revolutionary Unitarian Universalist Multicultural Ministries (DRUUMM).

By the time I entered my second semester of seminary, I was already on a first-name basis with people who were regarded as leaders in the movement. It was bizarre. Suddenly, at the age of fifty, Morales had become a very fashionable surname.

That spring I received a letter from UUA headquarters with a check for $600 to help with expenses for attending the 1997 General Assembly in Phoenix. During that GA, my first one, I was invited to be on a panel with other Latinx people at a workshop. I became part of the new Latino/a UU Networking Association (LUUNA). As a humorous aside, that may have been the first time in my life I was in a group with two people of Puerto Rican descent. Growing up in south Texas, I knew no Puerto Ricans. It speaks to the way other people's categories lump us together. In the category of the dominant culture, Puerto Ricans, Mexican Americans, Cubans, Bolivians, Guatemalans, and so forth, are all "Latinx" despite huge cultural differences. If you use "Hispanic," that throws in Spaniards too.

Two GAs later, in 1999 in Salt Lake City, I "walked" at the Service of the Living Tradition as a new minister in preliminary fellowship. I had just received a call to be the senior minister at Jefferson Unitarian Church in Golden, Colorado, at that time a congregation of four hundred members. At that same GA, the Unitarian Universalist Ministers Association had decided to add a position with an antiracism, anti-oppression, multicultural port- folio to its Executive Committee. After several more senior people declined to take the responsibility, I was asked to do it. I didn't even know what the UUMA Exec was! That threw me into the midst of all the politics of diversity and racism in the Association.

The whirlwind continued. Two years into my new ministry, I was recruited to be a nominee for the UUA Board of Trustees. At the end of a year on the UUA Board, I was asked to apply for the position of director of district services in Bill Sinkford's new administration. At this point, I was ending my third year as a parish minister. After some intense reflection, I decided to apply. I was selected, and I moved to Boston as a member of the administration's Leadership Council.

Let me summarize. It took only six years for me, a new semi- narian and a relatively new UU, to be appointed to the follow- ing positions: the Steering Committee of what was to become

*I am struck by how we are still doing the firsts. The first
Black UUMA Good Officer, the first Black president of
Starr King, the first Black president of the UUA, the first
Black minister at Shelter Rock—it should be no surprise
to us that we don't know the unwritten parts of the
system. We need to find ways to correct that.*

REV. DR. WILLIAM SINKFORD

DRUUMM, the Steering Committee of LUUNA, the UUMA
Executive Committee (during my first year in preliminary fellowship and as the first Latinx), the UUA Board of Trustees (as
the first Latinx), and the UUA's Leadership Council. Today I am
the first Latinx to serve as UUA president. It has seemed like
every time I walk through a door in this movement I have been
"the first."

The Invisible: Distorted Privilege, Presumption of Incompetence, and Distorted Relationships

A line from a play I saw a long time ago has stuck with me. One
character screamed at another, "I am not auditioning for a star-
ring role in your psychodrama!" It struck me because I sometimes
feel—and I know other ministers of color share this feeling—
that I am playing a role in our Association's collective psychodrama about race and ethnicity.

When typical Anglo ministers (in San Antonio, where I grew
up, we never used *Whites*, we always used *Anglo*) are asked to
serve in a leadership role in the UUMA or in the UUA, they can
assume they have been chosen because of their qualifications. *I
have never been able to assume that.* I never know if they want me

or if they want to punch the diversity card. I suspect it has often been the latter. Having a Latinx on a committee or a task force gives it political legitimacy.

Now I came into the UU movement in late middle age, after holding management positions in business and government and with a couple of graduate degrees. I have been a Fulbright lecturer in Spain and a Knight International Press fellow in Peru and so forth. It wasn't as though I had never accomplished anything or as if I had not been in positions of leadership; it wasn't as though I was not qualified for any of the positions I held.

And yet in no way would my qualifications have put me in line for the opportunities that were heaped upon me if I were White. A kind of *distorted privilege* was operating. I was caught up in a larger drama that I did not fully understand. I felt I was playing a role in someone else's psychodrama.

———

Sometimes you don't know you're not the right person for a position. One thing I have had to deal with in terms of being a good mentor, a good role model, is saying, "Listen, my friend, you want to be the number two in this big place over here, when your personality, your character, your heart and soul do not allow you to be a number two. You have to be number one. Find a smaller place." There's a reality check here in knowing what our qualifications are. When the institution puts us in the wrong place for the wrong reason because of whatever they're looking for, we often say yes, and sometimes when we don't even really want to do it.

REV. DR. HOPE JOHNSON

I want to speak to the question of qualifications. We need to be honest that we have such a small volunteer base in Unitarian Universalism that it's not just about Black people of color or Asians or Hispanics or Middle Eastern people. We have a lot of White people who are not that qualified for what they're doing either, so to put this all in racialized terms is a true disservice. We have many people who move into leadership rapidly because they are willing to serve. We know that in our congregations. They're breathing, and they're ready to serve. Our job is to make them better. That's what religious community is about, and that is a place where the dominant culture's paradigm continues to prevail. In my African-American tradition, you might have been a garbage man on the outside, but inside you ran the church because you were educated, trained, and given the ability. We are not, I hope, a community where everybody has to come in with their Harvard degree before they can do anything. We are here to be welcoming, and then to have people dismissed as unqualified and pulled in because of affirmative action because they were willing to give up their time and service for their faith—it's insulting. When I was installed at my congregation, I asked Rev. Carlton Smith to do my charge. He looked me straight in the eye and said, "There is no one more qualified than you." We should say that to each other often. "You are in this place because you have

earned it. You deserve it. You can do the job. There is no
one more qualified than you. There may be people as
qualified, but no one more. This is your place." I reject
that I have not earned where I am, and if other people
don't want to see that, that is their loss; but we need to lift
up and address how it makes us feel to be challenged about
our qualifications, how we may internalize a feeling of not
being qualified, how we may have that reflected back at
us, sometimes by us. How are we going to gain perspective
and reflection on those issues about the validity of our
call, and that we deserve to be where we are, and that
we deserve to be in even more places than we are?
How are we going to be confident about that? So I am
uncomfortable with the president of our denomination
saying things that will lead people to believe that I am in
my place as the first African-American woman minister at
my congregation because I am a token, because I am an
affirmative-action call. That is not the case. I went
through the search like everyone else. I succeeded a White
male minister who came to me and said, "You are
qualified for this position. You apply for this position."
We do need that internal confirmation that we went
through the process just like everybody else and we got
called. We can turn around and say, "I did just what
you did, and I'm here, so don't give me that."

REV. NATALIE MAXWELL FENIMORE

One thing I learned was that if one is a "minority" and reasonably competent, the offers of leadership positions in our movement never stop. We have to fight off a constant barrage of offers. I have seen this happen to a number of my minority colleagues.

The fact is that we "minority" religious professionals are offered opportunities and responsibilities not offered to others. This is what I mean by distorted privilege. Being from a minority group confers a limited privilege. It is the odd privilege of getting to take on additional assignments and the burden of always being the voice of Latinxs, Blacks, Asians, Native Americans, and more.

This dynamic has a negative side. As I mentioned above, I and other people of color never know whether "they" want us or whether they want a token. I am not sure whether the people who have asked me to serve really knew. What this means is that people of color participate in a way that is not truly equal, that is somehow tainted. We are never part of the group in the same way that others are. It can be infuriating.

There is another perverse dynamic as well. I call it the presumption of incompetence. In part because the UUA's hunger for diversity is so strong (and I share that hunger), a semiconscious devaluing of the participation of colleagues of color occurs. This is a natural and inevitable consequence of our affirmative action in reaching out for diversity. If people think I am serving on a committee or board primarily because I am Latino, it is a short step to assume that I am less qualified than other members. *Distorted privilege and the presumption of incompetence are two sides of the same coin.*

I am glad Unitarian Universalists strive for diversity. I strive for it in appointments I make. However, we are naive if we believe this does not distort and muddy relationships. It puts a burden, almost always an invisible psychic burden, on people of color. We hunger for relationships that are free of these distortions and uncertainties.

When I was serving as UUA president, I invited a couple of people to be kind of a clearness committee. That was enormously helpful. Within our faith, I did not have people of color to be colleagues with who were at anything like my level of responsibility. So I had to go outside. There are now enough of us who have been or are in positions of recognized, important, responsible leadership. There ought to be some way to leverage that, beyond the responsibility we all embrace of mentoring and sharing our wisdom.

REV. DR. WILLIAM SINKFORD

Archetypes

Categories can be necessary, but they are also oversimplifications that do subtle violence to the complex reality in which we all live and move. Once people are put into categories, archetypes are instantly created and people are judged by how closely they match the archetypes.

The archetype for a Latino is a short man with dark brown skin, black hair, and dark eyes, who speaks English, if at all, with an accent, and is poorly educated. To the extent that any of us deviates from the stereotype, we lose some legitimacy. I was recently in a meeting where a longtime colleague and good friend noted, with concern, that no people of color were in our working group. Shortly afterward this friend realized what he had done. He apologized privately and was quite embarrassed that he had not counted me as a person of color. I told him that I was not offended and that this happens to me all the time.

*We want to be visible in all our variety. We're often
telling our members, "Bring your full self into the room."
We've got to listen to that and bring our full selves to
meet them so that we'll be present in all our variety,
not labeled or determined. Our identities are our
own. They're all our own. They're all valid. We
don't have to prove that. Push boundaries.*

REV. NATALIE MAXWELL FENIMORE

There is ironic humor here. I don't know of a single ancestor on either side of my family without a Spanish surname (extended family names include Lopez, Sánchez, Esparza, Valdez, Esteban, Martinez, *ad infinitum*). Not a single one of my many aunts or uncles married a non-Latinx (all that changed with my generation). In that sense, I am as Latino or Hispanic as they come. Yet I don't fit the stereotype very well. My skin is too light (my father's family emigrated from eastern Spain and has fair skin). I

---

*Very few of the beautiful cadre of up-and-coming
religious professionals of color we see at Finding Our
Way Home are interested in parish ministry for all the
reasons that we've been talking about. They know the
struggles of those of us who've been in parish ministry
longer. They've heard the stories. They're not willing
to invest the time or deal with the headaches
or the hassles of doing this.*

REV. MANISH MISHRA-MARZETTI

speak English without an identifiable accent. I was fortunate to receive a rather elite education.

The cumulative effect of playing a role in someone else's drama is that we ministers of color (and this applies equally to religious educators, musicians, and lay leaders) are deprived of a piece of our humanity. We are often seen through the filters of the categories. Relationships get distorted. We cannot participate in the same way that others do.

―――――

As someone who is mentoring seminarians of color at Meadville, I want to offer support but also answer the question that one student asked: "Is there room for me in Unitarian Universalism?" It's hard to have to say, "Well, maybe," while wanting to say, "Yes, of course!" That difficult question keeps coming up: How do we mentor people trying to decide what they want to do, when we know the stories we know and with the pain we have seen and experienced? How do we nurture future religious professionals of color in the midst of this?

REV. DARRICK JACKSON

―――――

This is one reason that gatherings of religious professionals of color have been such powerful and important experiences. Every year we meet at a gathering aptly named Finding Our Way Home. At these meetings we belong in a fuller way. These colleagues *get it!* In these gatherings, we are more fully seen as human beings, not someone else's categories. People can lay down the burdens of the labels they have been forced to carry. The emotional and spiritual importance of Finding Our Way Home is hard to express.

We are so hungry to know one another and to be known for who we fully are. It is tragic and painful to see how far we still need to go in our movement.

Navigating the Contradictions

So how does one navigate all this?

The metaphor of playing a role in a drama is useful. I did a bit of acting in high school and college and in community theater, playing everything from a young lover in Shakespeare's *Taming of the Shrew* to rather silly parts in comedies to a Puritan judge condemning innocent people to hang in a college production of *The Crucible*. To play a role well, I had to throw myself into it, to try to become the character and see the world through their eyes. Of course, I am not any of the roles I played or play today. None of us is.

Ministry is different from theater though. We strive to bring our true selves to our ministries. Yet every one of us is also more than the role we play. I realize that I have no control over whether I am asked to play a given role. I cannot control to what extent my ethnicity is part of being chosen. I *can* control whether I choose to accept the role and how I play it. Right now I am the president of our Association. I chose to seek the position and perform that role as best I can. And I am more than my current role. I will be president for a short time; I will always be me.

Sociologists use the term *role distance* to describe this ability to see the roles we play in perspective. I believe role distance is essential to maintaining sanity. If we conflate ourselves with our roles, we literally lose perspective and can easily do harm to ourselves and the movement we serve.

For me, one critical way of maintaining perspective is nurturing relationships with people who know me outside my role—my family and my close friends. These relationships keep me

My family—my personal, biological, and chosen loved
ones—are what sustains me.

REV. NATALIE MAXWELL FENIMORE

————

grounded. One danger of the roles we play in ministry and religious leadership is that they can easily become so all-consuming that we neglect the very relationships that keep us grounded.

One final tactic that I have found invaluable is stubbornness. Oh, I could pretty it up and call it taking the long view, or being steadfast, strong, or courageous. But the truth is that when the madness in our movement around race and ethnicity has been most difficult for me, simple stubbornness has seen me through. (I can't imagine serving as UUA president without it!)

At its best, this stubbornness is a *faithful stubbornness*, grounded in both commitment and humility. *Commitment* is all about keeping faith with the beloved community of compassionate and authentic relationships that we are striving to create. Commitment is also about keeping faith with one another. Covenant, after all, is about commitments. *Humility* is the realization that we are not there yet, that we will not get there in our lifetimes. It's also a

————

Religious professionals of color need ministers
themselves. I believe in spiritual direction. It is not the
same as therapy. Both are valuable. For support, we
need someone who is an accountability person who is
not in our space. I cannot emphasize enough my belief
that these are the basis of healthy ministry for us.

REV. SOFIA BETANCOURT

*We all have some kind of privilege. We have privilege
by virtue of being religious leaders. We have to be
responsible to that if we want other people to be
responsible to it too. Unitarian Universalism lacks a
theology of humility. How do we balance that against
audacity, which is also important in our ministries? I
have been in institutional places of power for a relatively
short period of time, and I remember very viscerally not
being in the position of power that I'm in now. I do not
know how long it will last, but from everything that I
see—from my colleagues to my congregation to my
own heart to the span of my life—I do not expect it to last
long, so then the questions are: What am I doing now?
How am I making it worth it? What are we actually
going to do?*

REV. MITRA RAHNEMA

———

recognition of personal limitations. The beloved community does not depend on any one of us, and none of us will live there. But each one of us gets to visit. Faithful stubbornness is staying the course.

Looking Ahead: It's Complicated

Race still matters in America, and will continue to matter for the foreseeable future. Racism is like an infectious disease that has mutated and become resistant to treatment. Today's racism is less overt. It is more deceptive and more cunning. Fifty years ago in

Selma the suppression of Black voters was blatant. Today voter suppression uses gerrymandering and insidious legal barriers to make it harder both to register and to vote.

We UUs need to continue to help move the universe toward justice. Doing that today and tomorrow is going to require different tactics. America has changed dramatically in the last fifty years and will continue to change. Our old categories are a poor fit. So are our old strategies.

On a personal level this means we have to navigate our lives and identities in a different world. Our commitment to justice requires us to act with as much subtlety and agility as the proponents of ignorance and fear do. We have to be especially mindful of the way we use labels to put one another into boxes. The children entering elementary school today defy our old categories. Some urban school districts have children entering their system who speak more than a hundred different languages. We need to pay attention to understand the issues facing kids who are part Latinx and part Anglo, part Vietnamese and part African American, part Native American and part Pacific Islander, and so forth.

We especially need to be careful about how we use labels around race and ethnicity. Labels are necessary. We can't talk without them. We just need to remember that labels are like power tools. They help us point to injustice, create movements, and pass laws. We cannot speak truth to power without labels. Labels easily become weapons we use to cram people into our preconceived notions. Labels are how we force other people to play roles in our psychodramas. Labels always distort and simplify. That is what they are for. We just have to use them with care and learn to hold them lightly.

I don't want to ever tell someone what their identity is. That is oppressive. Sticking labels on people is a kind of violence. They should tell me what labels, if any, make sense to them. We should tell each other and listen to one another. In the beloved community we won't need to label each other, for we will know one another too deeply.

This isn't rocket science. This is about compassion and empathy. It is about paying attention. It is about having an open and a loving heart. It is about not being clueless. As always, if we allow it to, love will guide us.

RESPONSE TO PETER MORALES
Rev. Marisol Caballero

I LIKE TO JOKE, "I've been UU almost as long as I've been brown." In truth, I have been at this a long time. I understand the stereotypical expectations of how and who I should be with regard to my identity both as a Latina and as a Unitarian Universalist. I am also a woman, a lesbian, a proud Texan, and (many say) I look much younger than my thirty-six years. I have become adept at navigating this terrain. I have never understood myself as living anywhere other than at the intersection of such an unexpected combination of identities. Unitarian Universalists do not expect one of their ministers to be a Chicana/Tejana, to be young, loud, and boisterous. UUs do not expect a young Latina to be well spoken or well educated either, and I am both. Latinxs do not often expect me to be UU or an out lesbian. To complicate things all the more, the LGBTQ community, for the most part, does not expect me to be religious.

To embody the unexpected while living a bicultural life is a tricky business. This necessary survival skill is often referred to as code switching. To become ordained into ministry to and with a faith community that is largely White while existing in the skin of someone who defies expectations in each of my worlds takes mastery. Some days I believe I have this dance down, I can do it with my eyes closed. Most days I am left hoping that no one catches me making up the steps as I go along. Maybe if I smile enough, maybe if I am graceful enough, no one will notice when I stub my toe or trip on this bizarre, shape-shifting dance floor.

I wanted to talk about the question of wholeness as opposed to parts. I agree very much with this idea that our programs for religious education, faith formation, and spiritual development should be about developing a sense of yourself as a whole and not your various parts, and that we have to do a better job of attending to people's wholeness and not their various parts. For me personally, my Blackness is a whole that includes many cultures, many experiences, and many races in me, but that's whole for me in my Blackness. I don't parcel myself out, nor do I invite other people to parcel me out.

REV. NATALIE MAXWELL FENIMORE

———

The seminary and internship years are spent in conversation with professors and supervisors talking about making sure to convey this enigmatic thing called ministerial authority. We are advised, "Be authentic!" and "Be confident!" But all the self-assuredness in the world doesn't stand a chance when congregants are impressed to hear I really do write my own sermons, when they insist upon pronouncing my name incorrectly, and when they relate to me as an intern in churches that I have never served as intern ("You're going to make a great minister some day!" "That sermon was great! You are really growing!"). In seminary, I was not taught how to be "authentic" when I showed up to work grieving because yet another murderous police officer had escaped indictment, not only feeling utterly alone in my grief but also experiencing White hostility to my grief.

Maybe the paradox of the work of a minister of color is that we must love and truly care for our congregants. It would be dishonest to claim that we necessarily *like* all of them, but we must love them while simultaneously holding expectations of great things from their hearts and their courage and holding expectations that they will disappoint and break *our* hearts. I keep holding out the hope that I will meet a UU minster of color whose experience of ministry will be the exception. I want to believe that this is not what I've signed up for, because on most days, I truly feel at home in this work and in this faith. Doing the work of ministry, a complicated calling by nature, is further complicated by living in the tension of loving the people while expecting to be hurt by them. In any other relational structure, this would seem a dysfunctional, co-dependent, and perhaps abusive dynamic. It is no wonder Unitarian Universalism loses so many talented ministers of color to attrition. Not many would sign up to offer their hearts fully to guaranteed heartbreak.

———

When you expect more from folks, that's when the disappointment and the pain are greatest, because if you didn't care, it wouldn't bother you. Sometimes we let our friends and acquaintances off easily because they say, "I didn't mean it that way," or "You know I would never intentionally hurt you." But no matter whether it is a stab to the heart or a superficial wound, a wound is a wound is a wound. And people can say, "Sticks and stones may break my bones but words will never hurt me," but words can kill your spirit.

REV. DR. SUSAN NEWMAN MOORE

In a way, I think the more pastoral response is to challenge the person. It's worth challenging the notion that the sidestepping route is more pastoral. It's gentler, but I don't think the gentler thing is always more pastoral. I don't think it's always the right thing to do, because self-care is equally important. Sometimes I just have to say, "I don't want to walk into this with you. I can't do this. I can't go there."

REV. LAUREN SMITH

There's a Zen phrase "How we do anything is how we do everything." If we all are being treated this way, what's happening with people who walk in through our doors? This is about Unitarian Universalism, and that's why it's important to stand up for each other and change the dominant paradigm so we can grow Unitarian Universalism.

AISHA HAUSER

———

Tokenism and Internalized Racial Oppression versus Distorted Privilege

Yes, I have experienced the opening up of opportunities and invitations to leadership that Peter refers to as "distorted privilege," and his observations of the presumptions of incompetence as its flip side are right on the money, both with my own experience and with what I have heard anecdotally from other ministers of color within our movement. I do, however, disagree in terming this a *distorted privilege*, as I understand White privilege to refer not only to personal opportunity offered to White people individually but also to the cultural and institutional standards that favor Whiteness and White cultural expression as the norm.

Cultural and institutional racism within our movement and its subsequent internalized racist messages cause ministers of color, myself notwithstanding, to doubt our place within Unitarian Universalism, and that cannot be considered a privilege or an unfair advantage over a White colleague. It is no privilege, distorted or otherwise, to wonder if such opportunities are being granted us due to a true appreciation for our gifts of ministry or for the purposes of stroking the collective ego of those who see diversity as the goal rather than true healing from the damage racism inflicts upon *every one of us*. And it certainly does not feel as if ministers of color are being unduly privileged over our White colleagues when we are asked to serve in positions of leadership only to find out that (a) we have been asked to be a representative for our entire ethnicity, (b) our lone voice will be often and easily dismissed by the majority, and (c) a dedication toward effecting racial equity within Unitarian Universalism quickly brings a White colleague the status of "prophetic voice" but guarantees a minister of color a reputation as a troublemaker with a large-scale chip on the shoulder.

Like *reverse racism*, the term *distorted privilege* can become a dangerous one, its original meaning effortlessly misconstrued and used as ammunition by those hoping to say, "See. *That's* why so-and-so has such a padded resume! *I* should've been on the such-and-such committee. *I* should've been on that board. It's not fair. I'm being treated poorly because I'm White." Indeed, in the course of our careers, many of us have heard versions of this lament by White colleagues and congregants alike. The one true distortion in Peter's argument is the misuse of the word *privilege* to describe the epic mind game that is tokenism, when in reality

There's a difference between privilege and tokenism. It's not a privilege to be held in high demand for unpaid volunteer positions. That is not a privilege. That's tokenism. All we have to do is look within Unitarian Universalism at who's holding the highest salary levels and best paid positions. Who, in turn, is holding the secondary positions, tertiary positions, part-time ministry positions—the lower paying jobs? Where do professionals of color fall within this spectrum? All you have to do is that calculus and you can get a very good sense of where ministers who identify as multicultural and of color are situated. That is very, very apparent.

REV. MANISH MISHRA-MARZETTI

the notion of *White privilege* refers to the luxury of not having to wonder if treatment by White people (whether such treatment offers a perceived advantage or disadvantage) has anything to do with race or ethnicity over any other factor.

White Fragility

Tokenism is not a privilege but rather an indication that Unitarian Universalism remains a predominantly White movement that is generally awkward in its interacting with people of color. This awkwardness points to the majority of (White) Unitarian Universalists' inexperience in thinking or talking about racialization and racism, in living among or interacting with people of color, and in understanding themselves as negatively affected by the disease of racism. Both in the pulpit and in our pews,

Unitarian Universalists must be careful about how we talk about racism and the experience of UUs of color. We must take precautions in choosing our words so that our vocabulary about the disease of racism works to honor the true experience of UUs of color while honoring the ability of White UUs to be challenged on this issue and yet survive. I worry that the way we often choose to talk about the racism within our movement is more concerned with what has come to be known as White fragility than with truth telling. To tell the truth, I am tired. I am confident in saying that UU ministers of color are tired. This is a tired conversation. I would much rather focus the full array of my talents on other areas of ministry than continue to shine light on our movement's racism problem.

But as Peter notes, racism is a treatment-resistant disease that we must continue to fight nonetheless. I disagree that racism is now less overt. It continues to be both physically and spiritually deadly in its might. The problem is, rather, that the virus continues to mutate and, with each new mutation, has been left as an open wound to fester while the majority White folks, bothered by the sight and smell of it, deny the obvious trauma or merely avert their eyes.

Strategic Resolve

Like Peter, I am not going anywhere anytime soon. Maybe stubbornness is a Texan thing! My hope and inspiration lie in the knowledge that I am in good company with the multitude of the UUs of color and our White allies who place our faith in Unitarian Universalism's highest potential. Unitarian Universalism is my home, and I must work to help it realize its highest potential. Although love will surely guide us, it is not all we need. Strategic religious education, at every age and in every aspect of our religious life, is necessary to ensure the success of this work.

Ministers of color cannot be relied upon to cultivate the culture of humility required of this work when it is done with sincerity. Humility is not something that comes easily to religious liberals. We have delusions of it but not-so-secretly believe we are the answer to the world's problems.

I have no reservations in saying that ministers of color are largely ineffective in teaching White UUs to care about how they and others are affected by racism. I wish this weren't the case. God knows, like many of us, I have been doing the work of anti-racism, antioppression, and multiculturalism education and activism within this movement for many years and have made a small impact. But by and large, I have witnessed the greater majority of White UUs demonstrate no concern beyond listening to the occasional Sunday sermon on the topic of racism.

If I could, who is to say I wouldn't do the same? It has been tremendously heartening to see White UUs beginning to understand and wrestle with the necessity of the Black Lives Matter movement. Not far beneath my hard-learned cynicism, I am an

---

We need to find a place of spiritual life and balance so that we can have support and resources to ride through the ups and downs. What I crave most of all is a community of people of color who lead from strength, who are strength resources for one another, who are not talking the language of vulnerability. I've been vulnerable since I was born. I'm tired of that. I want to be strong. I want all of you to help me to be strong, to lead with strength, to be attracted to my strength like I'm attracted to yours. That's what I want for all of us.

REV. NATALIE MAXWELL FENIMORE

optimist at heart. Maybe someday, White UUs will cultivate spiritual and emotional investment in one another, truly understand that racial justice work begins with oneself, and see how much they have to personally gain from it, that they aren't merely doing me (and other people of color) a favor by devoting some of their time and energy to this work. All this is complicated, to say the least.

Thank goodness for organizations like DRUUMM, gatherings such as Finding Our Way Home, and allies like the Committee for Anti-racism, Anti-oppression, and Multiculturalism. No one strategy, curriculum, or sermon will guarantee UUs of color (ministerial or lay) a spot at the proverbial table. We are prepared to either elbow our way in or count our losses and leave. Likewise, no one strategy, curriculum, or sermon will convince the majority of White UUs to truly care about this fact and invest in bringing about change. I am grateful knowing that none of us has to figure this out on our own. I stand on the shoulders of giants and pray only that mine will prove sturdy enough that someday I can contribute to this struggle, a struggle that is long, tedious, painful, and arduous, but as necessary and worthwhile as any effort could be.

TRUST THYSELF

Rev. Walter LeFlore

GROWING UP IN upstate New York, I knew racism existed. I saw it and experienced it firsthand. I remember being mortified as I ran home to avoid a fight with several third- or fourth-graders who were calling me a nigger. I wanted to defend myself and fight if necessary, but being beaten up would have added insult to injury—or vice versa, more accurately. My always wise and sometimes patient mother heard my story and simply said, "Sometimes a good run is better than a bad stand." Lessons were learned!

My uncle's house in Mobile, Alabama, had been bombed three times before I reached the age of ten. He was a prominent civil rights activist.

I learned about racism the way our culture has taught us to think about racism. I understood it to be about individual behavior, the way one thought and acted, primarily people of lesser education, lesser character, and primarily, but certainly not exclusively, people who lived in the South. I didn't come to understand institutional racism until I was in my late twenties.

My first corporate work experience was with a major computer company, in the Human Resources department. My colleagues and I worked long, hard hours. We socialized together. Demographically, about 2 percent of the Human Resources folks were Black, 60-70 percent were White women, and the remainder were White men. But although I was among friends and I was fast-tracked with regular promotions and stock grants, I couldn't be comfortable with the fact that my predominantly White colleagues were better situated than I was to rise in the organization. After about three years, I found myself getting burned out.

The top level HRA manager suggested I spend some time with two Black external consultants who were working in another division on issues of "valuing diversity." I worked with Mike Brown and Price Cobbs for two or three years, initially on my own personal and professional development and later as consultants for my business units. Price, a nationally known psychiatrist who specializes in ethno-therapy, co-authored the seminal work *Black Rage.* Mike and Price helped me to better understand issues of race and to recognize the process and mechanisms of systemic racism within an otherwise congenial environment. That awareness has had a profound impact on the rest of my life.

So how might systemic, institutional racism play out in our predominantly White Unitarian Universalist congregations? What happens when a congregation calls a minister of color? Whatever the "correct" answer, it's likely different from what happens when a White minister is called, one who more closely represents the majority of Unitarian Universalists.

An important factor is the degree to which a minister of color is perceived to be "different." The greater the perceived difference— in color (degree of darkness), style (often noted as degree of stereotypic behavioral traits), class identification (or perception thereof), or use of "proper" language—the more that difference will affect how that minister is received.

What may be of greatest importance is how comfortable that minister is in their own skin while in that environment. This comfort can be the result of a strong sense of self, a strong sense of belonging, and skill and confidence at navigating a predominantly middle- to upper-middle-class White environment.

We Asians contend with the model minority myth—that
we're this high-achieving group of people who don't
cause trouble, don't stir the pot. These assumptions kick
in with Asian Americans, and what happens is the
unspoken assumption that "Well, you're practically like
us." Then the "practically" part gets further glossed over:
"You are us. You are just like us." There's a lot that's lost.
It's only within the past year that I've started wearing
Indian clothing (kurtas) in professional settings, and it's
a very intentional choice for me. It's a reclaiming of my
cultural identity and a gentle reminder: Maybe I don't
have an accent, maybe I've got a pedigree that you like,
the academic credentials that you like, but I am from a
different family background. I am from a different
cultural background. It's my way of trying to gently assert
that. Even then I have to think about it. I just began a
new ministry, and I still wear a kurta on occasion, but I
have to think about it. Is it "acceptable" at this stage in
my ministry to do that in a given context? That's part of
the complexity each of us has to navigate. Somehow
there's a politics and a diplomacy to just being ourselves,
and that's hard, but that's the reality.

REV. MANISH MISHRA-MARZETTI

There are a number of other factors that can affect the minister of color's experience: Are the potential ramifications of a minister of color the elephant in the room, or is the manifestation of differences anticipated so that the community can openly and honestly address any issues that may surface or lurk in the background? Who is responsible for raising the issue of difference when it is perceived as a possible dynamic in the congregation's everyday life? Do both the minister and the congregation understand that issues of authority, perceptions of competence or performance, and expectations of the minister may well be affected by dynamics of difference? Does at least one party to this dance of relationship recognize and understand these dynamics, and are they competent at navigating the turbulent and muddy waters of difference, especially differences based on race?

These are significant issues when a minister of color works within a predominantly White congregational setting. Ministers

---

We need to claim power, learn about power and its uses, and develop our own professional skills inventory, knowing what we do and leading with a certainty about our own skills and abilities, no matter what other people think. No matter what we've got to prove, we know what we're doing once we're there. And we don't want to be set up for failure, so be clear about what you do, know the system in which you operate, who the power brokers are, whether or not you choose to engage with it. Don't choose from ignorance. We should support each other in making sure we all know as much as possible.

REV. NATALIE MAXWELL FENIMORE

of color must be prepared to address them when we minister within Unitarian Universalism. I want to set aside the go-to issue of competence. We can't become fellowshipped without having demonstrated competence while navigating our rigorous credentialing process. Yes, we all have areas in which we can and should improve, but this should not be confused with issues of competence.

Rather, I want to focus on what I understand to be the two most salient attributes of being a successful minister of color in our denomination: self-knowledge and preparation.

Know Thyself

Power is what is needed to create change, and ministers are fundamentally about creating change. That power can come from many different personal traits, including race, age, gender, education, savvy, and personal style. Power is seldom granted to those who are seen as other. To the extent that White privilege and its corollary, racism, are at play, we are not likely to be granted authority or power to any significant degree. My contention is that these dynamics are always in play in our culture to one degree or another. Rather than wait for time to heal all wounds or to hope for the best, a more proactive approach is to leverage the inherent authority of the position of minister while simultaneously cultivating relationships.

Cultivating genuine relationships requires a high degree of authenticity. Authenticity requires a high level of knowledge and understanding of who one is and an awareness of who one professes to be but is not. Training in seminary and internships goes a long way toward providing such clarity. Throughout the process we are told that self is the foundation of who one is as a minister. To be successful and, more importantly, to survive ministry, one must be aligned and comfortable with oneself.

While it may not be true for all of us, I know my training and years of formal ministerial development did not grant me much opportunity to explore issues of internalized racism. I strongly suspect the same is true for most people of color in our denomination. During my several years of formal development in seminary, work experiences, and internship, I can count on one hand the number of times I've been asked to address my relationship to my racial identity. Even then it came in the form of a question something like, "How will being a minister of color affect your ministry?" or "What's it going to be like being a minister of color in our denomination?"—a simple, open-ended question with little or no direction or encouragement to dig deeper. Perhaps it was for the best, as I doubt the questioners were ready to hear how devastatingly lonely it would probably be. Inevitably the answer was accepted at face value. Besides, issues of race were almost always addressed in terms of the White population; people of color were "them" and systemic racism was "out there."

It wasn't until I was almost halfway through my summer-long, full-time clinical pastoral education program that I came face to face with myself, with questions like: How did I deal with significant loss, with death, risk, and discomfort? How open was I willing to be with my supervisor and peers about my frailties, inadequacies, fears, hopes, and desires? What significant experiences in my life, good and bad, helped mold me? What, in total honesty, was my relationship with my family? Where and when had I experienced failure and success? What had I learned about myself?

No doubt race and racism were embedded in many of these analyses. But I don't believe I explored my internalized relationship with my race nearly as deeply as I explored learning to be a non-anxious presence or how my theology affected my ability to minister to people with a very different frame of reference from my own.

People of color are impeded in finding our authenticity until we have found and dislodged the cultural, racist, stereotyping perceptions of us that we have unwittingly internalized. Just as we learn to sit with a dying person as a non-anxious presence, can we learn to sit with ourselves as a non-anxious presence in regard to issues of race and racism? If not, we will always be in reactive mode, not proactively driven by self-comfort and maximized options.

Experience convinces me that as people of color, we have a very real need to deeply analyze the impact of a culture that tends to dehumanize and categorize us before seeing us as individuals, that tends to define us in reference to a deficit model. How could we not see ourselves as "other" when we live in a world that conditions us all to see White people as normative? How can we see ourselves living and working in an environment in which most of the people we interact with do not look like us, do not share our generalized historic cultural experiences, and may unconsciously devalue us? And more painfully, how can we see ourselves living and working with people who do not see us as "real" UUs after all our dollars and years spent to become credentialed UU ministers!

We have to deeply grapple with and rigorously analyze these salient questions if we are to find our authentic selves. These are not issues UU institutions tend to have any competency to address. White people are the primary reference point in American culture, society, and churches. UU programs and trainings are almost exclusively focused on what White people need to learn, do, or change in order to have a more just society. And yes, some of that is to be more accepting of differences that may be manifested by people of color.

That may be fine as far as it goes, but it does not address the need for people of color to grapple in a deep way with the nature and ramifications of being defined as other, seeing ourselves as other, often feeling not included or unsupported by the community we have learned to love. It does not address how we of color get our spiritual needs met in a culture that is excessively cerebral. It does not address the universal human need to belong, to be seen, to be accepted.

As people and ministers of color, we have a unique dilemma: how to be open and available to our primarily White parishioners, who may fail to see the fullness of who we are, who may push and pull us to adapt to their normative culture, to fit in. It is often difficult to be vulnerable in an environment that all too often feels hostile to who and what we are. Yet this is our chosen faith, our chosen profession.

These are issues that have their genesis in the larger culture but affect us directly as they play out in UU congregations. We need to be able to navigate these waters and not just survive but also thrive. Assessing the impact on us of living in a fundamentally racist culture is a significant piece of work we need to do for ourselves, for our well-being and to find our authentic selves. We need to get comfortable leveraging our legitimate ministerial authority and personal power to make space for the fullness of who we are. And that is a fundamentally different approach than elbowing others aside in order to make space for ourselves.

Being Prepared

While our congregations might like to believe that UUs are different from the wider culture, the truth is that we are a part of it and participate in it. Yes, we have a particular Unitarian Universalist culture, but nonetheless, it reflects a White, male, upper-middle-class, well-educated orientation. For most people of color, it's a culture that is not likely to feel wholly our own; nor is it a culture we're automatically assumed to be part of.

In addition, it's important to acknowledge and understand that our UU culture tends to act as if, even believe, that race is

We're talking about a religion that is still part of the culture we live in. If we were bankers, we'd still be talking about how we couldn't get past the VP position. If we were in journalism, we couldn't get on the national news. This is my third career. There's no career I've been in where I haven't had to have this conversation. A whole group of us at the New York Times called ourselves the Posse, and we could sit in the cafeteria and talk about where we couldn't work yet at the Times. So I just want us to remember that this is a societal issue. I think it's more painful for us because we're a faith tradition, and our highest and best aspirations should be brought to bear on everything we do. It certainly hurts me. But we're still in the United States of America. We know how that's been turning out. We're still as vulnerable to the illness of American culture as anyone else. Our faith inoculates us a little bit, but not completely. We can't imagine there would be someplace better, because there's nowhere else we could go where we wouldn't be having this conversation. Nowhere. So we might as well stay here and have it with each other.

REV. ROSEMARY BRAY MCNATT

not a salient issue in our liberal institution, which often defines itself as "welcoming." (It should be noted that our welcoming program was designed to be welcoming of LGBT people and may not be fully transferable to other dimensions of diversity.) Therefore, people of color often find themselves in an institutional environment that does not acknowledge the impact of race, racism, or oppression. The person of color may be the only one in the room who recognizes (or anticipates) that a racial dynamic is at play.

If this added dimension, or at least its potential, is not openly acknowledged, it often falls to the person of color to name the dynamic or to acquiesce to a generalized interpretation that simply is not real. Either way, there may be significant risk. The choice is often between bringing more attention to one's difference or having one's difference treated as if it doesn't exist except as an aspect of personality.

As in the larger culture, when a person who is defined as different, by whatever definition, names the unspoken or questions a norm, they are often marginalized. The in-group tends to coalesce around their sameness and challenge the validity of the question or observation, perhaps even the acceptability of the person who has spoken up.

Most people of color learn this critical lesson through experience. We learn that we have to be prepared to make conscious choices about when and how to deal with resistance to our difference. We often make the false assumption that not rocking the boat is a safe choice. It may or may not be. Significant risks may lurk in the unacknowledged. Specifically, "difference" is often perceived and interpreted as personal defect.

It's a given that raising the issue of race makes some people uncomfortable, even defensive. This is a particular risk in an environment of smart, accomplished, well-meaning people who are used to being in charge and right. If persons of color experience

We're all in jeopardy until something changes.
Not to understand how power structures work is
ultimately folly in any system. We are not the only
organization that has this mess on its hands. It
happens in academia. It happened when, all of a
sudden, there were all these appointees of color
at administrative levels, most of whom were
incompetent, so that the White people who
appointed them could say, "We gave you what
you wanted, and look what you got."

REV. DR. ORLANDA BRUGNOLA

---

discomfort as a result of their difference and do not acknowledge it, unhappy consequences are likely. If a White person or group is questioned about issues of race, they often react defensively. The larger culture's operative default is that we of color are expected to not feel discomfort, but if we do, we are to get over it, because the in-group shares consensus that it couldn't be the result of the environment (and even if it is, "things are getting better").

Being prepared as people of color means maintaining constant awareness that beyond the words spoken or the content of the issue on the table, interpersonal dynamics are always at play. The dynamics probably involve issues of inclusion and exclusion, superiority and inferiority, power and authority. Race, class, gender, and other areas of difference are probably always at play in our interpersonal and group dynamics because they are an inescapable part of the larger culture we live in. The issue is often not whether but to what degree these issues are alive in our congregational interactions.

Being prepared as people of color means operating on the assumption that issues of systemic difference are at play in all our interactions to one degree or another, manifesting in both obvious and subtle ways. I'm suggesting that people of color operate on the assumption that race is always an active dynamic, or potentially so. Sometimes issues of difference can have beneficial impact, but too often the impact is harmful.

Raising an issue that is not already seen (or acknowledged) often becomes an issue all its own. This is particularly true in regard to issues of race and racism. When I use the term *racism*, I am not talking about personal animosity or one person's antipathy toward a person of color. Rather, I'm referring to a societal dynamic that privileges White, Eurocentric normative structures over all others. This is a societal dynamic that we as individuals absorb in some fashion by dint of being part of the culture, whether we are White or people of color. It's in the air we breathe and often goes unnoticed.

It's no small thing to raise an issue having to do with race and racism; it can make one the focus of ill ease, defensiveness, even marginalization. The dynamic of privilege may be active in a conversation that White participants perceive has having nothing to do with race, but pointing it out can be disruptive and completely disorienting to them. Therefore, it's essential for people of color to have tools to address issues of race and racism without having to name it or have others concur with our assessment.

Truth be told, there are times when it is more advantageous to not address the issue directly. In an environment where there appears to be limited understanding or acknowledgment of issues of race and racism, raising the subject can commit one to long and often arduous conversations that may do nothing but drive all parties further apart. If we are operating in an environment already troubled by contentious issues, raising such issues as race and racism is probably not to anyone's short-term benefit.

White privilege connotes superiority, whether acknowledged or not. It is manifested in a presumption of correct positions, an assumed right to set the rules of interaction, an expectation of acquiescence on the part of the person of color, and a belief that all should fit into the established normative structure. These dynamics often manifest for people of color as racism, and they are generally system-wide rather than particular to individual people or just the mean-spirited or shortsighted ones.

It is possible, even preferable at times, to address issues of race and racism indirectly, to engage the issue on a different playing field. Legitimate authority can be leveraged to enhance one's power in an organizational system. We need to understand quite

———

It can be more comfortable to talk about the behavior of white people in positions of power and less comfortable to talk about people of color in positions of power. What happens when we're moving into these roles? There's a lot of negative feeling about power within Unitarian Universalism. It gets a rap, and that power isn't necessarily negative. One way we deal with power is to reject that we have it. That happens across the board regardless of race and cultural background, and one thing that happens when we negate and fail to claim the power we have is that we put ourselves in a position to abuse it. How do we deal with entering into this dynamic as people of color?

REV. LAUREN SMITH

clearly that authority and power are not the same. Change requires some form of power (energy) be applied.

An individual's power can stem from their official position and/or their personality style. For example, the congregational matriarch often wields a considerable amount of power. Tenure, personal relationships, and personal style are often enough to allow that person to have sufficient power to affect decisions and "the way we do things around here." White privilege is often leveraged to enhance personal power. Someone else who may chair an important committee, especially a person of color, may have much less ability to influence outcomes, even though they hold a position of authority. Fighting this dynamic on a person-to-person or issue-to-issue basis is often fraught with disappointment. It can lead to a sense of disempowerment, which can easily lead to a sense of futility or failure, which in turn can lead to anger, which can prompt striking out. Needless to say, a good outcome is unlikely for anyone.

To help level the playing field, we as people of color need to insist on occupying our rightful place in the organization, not suffer quietly. The position of minister comes with legitimate authority that is inherent in being trained, credentialed, and called. Leveraging the authority inherent in the position can shift the focus away from right and wrong, my personal preference versus yours, my personal style versus yours or theirs.

By emphasizing position, we have a better chance of occupying our rightful places in our organizations while at the same time wrestling with the subtleties of White privilege. The position of minister can then be dealt with as an issue separate from race, separate from personality. It becomes an issue ostensibly about the role and authority of minister. With a primary focus on the position, we put up a buffer against the leverage and power of systemic White privilege.

I invite us to claim our audacity, to claim our ambition,
to push outside the box, to move into a different pay
scale, a different level of responsibility, and to be in a
position at a congregation where people listen when we
talk. That means, for me, stepping up into, and not
allowing myself to think small about, myself and my
ministry. I feel that I do this in many ways in honor of
my mother. She did not take the Greyhound bus out of
Alabama for me to play small. I would be completely
disrespecting her, my grandmother, and everybody I
know if I didn't move myself out of the expected and
comfortable places, because they did not stay in the
expected and comfortable places. I feel responsible to
that. I have to take my place on that journey, and I can't
let other people's small-mindedness about where I should
be and what I can and cannot do dictate my actions.

REV. NATALIE MAXWELL FENIMORE

In the largely anti-authority culture of Unitarian Universalism, a focus on the inherent authority of the position of minister is likely to engender resistance. Ministers of color should take that as a given and be prepared to ride out the various ways this resistance gets played out. (Such resistance is seldom avoided, in any event.) Unfortunately, there is a catch-22: Too often we need to be in closer relationship with individuals and the congregation before conversations concerning race and racism are likely to be profitable.

The dynamics of organizational systems often dictate that we are granted "in-ness" by virtue of our positions, personal relationships, longevity, or all three before we are "entitled" to question, challenge, and address issues of race and racism. It is therefore critical that, as part of being prepared to minister to a largely White congregation, we learn the importance of finding or creating allies. This is true for anyone to be successful in any group, but it is especially true for people of color, and even more so for Black men, who carry a particular stigma.

———

I have this in my history: dealing with anger and not wanting to be the angry Black man but also fulfilling the ministerial role and having to take care of the White people. I'm caught between the stereotypes. I'm trying to find another way, and I can't always find it. That's a struggle I often deal with.

REV. DARRICK JACKSON

———

All too often in American society, Black men are put in a peculiar place of being seen as a threat in some form. We need to be intentional about resisting being placed or kept in that box. Black men in particular walk a razor's edge between claiming ministerial authority, which bumps up against UU resistance to authority, and owning our Black maleness, which bumps up against a cultural fear of Black men.

Many women attest to being ignored in meetings with men present, to making a suggestion that is not heard or valued until the same suggestion is made by a male. So too, Black men are often perceived as intimidating or arrogant. Better such interpretations be redirected to the position of minister, which has inherent legitimacy, than to the personality of the individual who is perceived as different.

Another issue of importance that is sorely missing in our ministerial development and that I have chosen not to address in more depth in this essay is knowledge of group dynamics and how systems tend to operate. It is important for us as ministers and people of color to know how to navigate systems; to know how to find, identify, and make use of systemic strengths and weaknesses; and to know where the leverage points are that have the greatest potential for creating positive change.

———

I want to talk about the vulnerability of those of us in "hire-to-call" positions. When stuff went nuts in my congregation a few years ago, the Board said that I worked for them. I had to remind them that they were the elected representatives and I was the called minister and together we work for the congregation. You can't do that when you're hire-to-call. If I could wave a magic wand, I would make hire-to-call disappear, because it undermines our authority as ministers and it's extremely dangerous for people of color. If we can manage to be in the search process and manage to get called, it places us on a firmer foundation when trouble happens, and trouble's coming.

REV. ROSEMARY BRAY MCNATT

One temptation for me is to treat maneuvering through the structures of Unitarian Universalism as a power question. How do I understand the powers and the principalities so that I can prevent them from manipulating me? And I find that deeply offends my sense of why I was called into ministry. I hope I never get over the sense of being offended by that.

REV. DR. WILLIAM SINKFORD

———

When we ministers of color have done our ministerial development and have assessed who and what we are, we can then trust ourselves to meet any life circumstance we face. When we have a deep sense of self-knowledge and self-comfort, we can truly trust ourselves to wade in the water of Unitarian Universalist ministry.

Response to Walter LeFlore
Rev. Dr. Kristen Harper

TAYLOR BRANCH, author of *Parting the Waters: The King Years*, wrote, "Almost as color defines vision itself, race shapes the cultural eye—what we do and do not notice, the reach of empathy and the alignment of response."

"Did you see the watermelon?" I asked my husband. We were on Candidating Week and I was looking around the beautiful room where we were to stay while we got to know the congregation better. We had been left a bunch of food to snack on between meals. A large watermelon was prominently displayed on the table.

"Yeah," Jay said. "I saw it."

"Do you think they got it for us because we're Black?" I asked.

"I don't know. Why don't you ask them?" my helpful husband replied.

"I can't do that! They'd never call me."

There are moments in ministry when you realize you are perceived as different from everyone around you. As Walter remarks, "The greater the perceived difference . . . the more that difference will affect how that minister is received." They are moments when the fried chicken is placed in front of you at the potluck, or when members assume that you must be from the city or that you listen to rap music, when racist remarks are made and you are caught up short and unprepared. These moments can be very disconcerting, and knowing how to navigate them is key.

I was adopted into a White Unitarian Universalist family that taught me to love who I am as a Black woman and to appreciate and feel connected to a Black history of resilience, justice, and struggle. As a young girl, my mother dubbed me a truth teller, as I always speaking out against injustice. I had a voice long before I knew that as a term of empowerment. I grew up alongside a White New England culture that I learned to negotiate but that would never fully accept me. In the church I now serve, I consistently lift up the message that you can bring all of yourself to the table, and yet it has been clear for most of my life and my ministry that my Black self is, at best, tolerated by most. It isn't that the congregations I've served haven't respected me or cared for me. They have. It's just that many members wanted me to

---

I had this strange experience once of going into a religious education setting and talking about growing up in a Black community, and then I realized, as I was looking at some of the White faces there, that the children were having all kinds of pictures in their heads about what that looked like because they didn't experience it. That community I grew up in was a multi-everything community. I have a very broad community, combining people of every color in this room, lighter and darker, and some of those people were all in the same family. I know exactly where the White people in my family are, and that was not something we set aside. We incorporated that into what we were, what we are, because we are a hybrid people, and often what I celebrate is the strength that comes from having access to the best of everything.

REV. NATALIE MAXWELL FENIMORE

reflect their values, life experiences, and spirituality. And in many ways I do. But in some important ways I don't.

Being raised in a White family doesn't mean I think I am White or want to be White. I love being a Black woman, and the experiences of racism, exclusion, survival, and celebration that have pervaded my life help me to connect to the pain, anger, helplessness, and fear, as well as the need for hope and joy that so many people feel living in this broken world. There are few situations that I have not been prepared to be present to, because of the pain, anger, helplessness, and fear I have experienced as a Black woman.

I must state from the outset that some of my experiences are deeply commingled with being a young Black female who grew up in the Unitarian Universalist movement and connected strongly with the youth and young adult movements. In some situations, even now at forty-seven, I have wondered whether I would experience the same shutdown and dismissal if I were older. For example, for a while I brought chanting and clapping and stomping to the services I led, trying to encourage movement and feeling as I experienced in the Black churches I attended. This was met with not-so-quiet resistance and resentment. I love the old hymns I grew up with, but I also want to clap and shout and vibrate with rhythm. Music is one of the few ways I feel connected to spirit, to the divine, to others. This is something the young adults and youth of color I have worked alongside taught me.

Being prepared for "some resistance to our difference," as Walter states, isn't as easy as it sounds. We are desperately wanted by White UUs because we are seen as both the embodiment of their values of welcome and justice and exotic keys to spiritual discovery. This initial welcome feels genuine and feeds something in us that some of us have been looking for all our lives—a place where we belong. They lift us up but then discard us when we don't play nice, are used up, or are not what they expect.

What I get is exoticism. People react to me with this longing, this inner yearning to be taught. There's this "guru energy" I'm supposed to embody just by being alive as a person with Indian ancestry. Depending on our identity and our cultural or racial background, we get different responses evoked from the majority culture. That's a valuable thing for us and those coming after us to be thinking about: What is being evoked by our presence, and how are we politically, diplomatically, and professionally navigating what is being evoked?

REV. MANISH MISHRA-MARZETTI

———

For a year in my late teens, I attended a Black Baptist church to find a faith community where I could fit in and be accepted. However, I quickly discovered I couldn't bring my whole self there either. I wasn't Black enough. I didn't talk or act or wear my hair and clothes like the Black community there wanted me to. I didn't leave because they rejected me or because I realized I was theologically way too liberal for them; I left because I found their homophobia abhorrent. But it was the co-minister of that church who first suggested I go into ministry.

Walter writes, "People of color often find themselves in an institutional environment that does not acknowledge the impact of race, racism, or oppression." Nothing is more disheartening and dehumanizing than having your reality dismissed, your experience denied. Early on in my ministry when I would lift up the racial dynamics at play in a given situation, I would often be told I was mistaken, too sensitive, or projecting my own issues onto the situation. I learned quickly that most people experienced my comments as an attack on their character and could not listen to the pain or simple discomfort that I was experiencing. Although it went against everything I ever believed, I began to repress my feelings about all the incidents of racism and exclusion I experienced. What I once had believed was a strength—my truth telling—became a reason to dismiss me further and to ignore my leadership. I began to sacrifice my voice for my ministry.

Although Walter argues that navigating and passing the Association's credentialing and ordination process demonstrates our competence, I have found that not everyone in our congregations agrees with this. I have been asked if I write my own sermons or if the UUA prepares them for me. I want to joke with people who say such things and say to them, "Yes, the UUA has a sermon writer on staff. She's a young black woman." But mostly I feel diminished. I experience a lot of what I would call questions of competency. Often when I give advice on finance or management or process, I feel completely ignored. I wonder if this is a race or age or gender issue. They all intersect in me.

———

We keep touching on this question: "How can I be your minister when I need to tell you a difficult truth?" I say call a consultant. We don't do that enough. We are often the ones who are transported everywhere else to do the hard things. I want to remind us that when a consultant comes into our classroom or congregation or community, then we can still be a pastor or organizer or teacher. And sometimes we can't be both. If our colleagues can call on us to be accountable, why can't we call on each other?

REV. SOFIA BETANCOURT

I agree with Walter that growing relationships and building alliances is the most effective step to address race and racism in our congregations. When you have ministered with people during their most painful moments, when you have buried their loved ones and held their hands through their grief, when you have walked with them through a painful divorce or breakup, people are more likely to grant you the authority you need to raise the tricky issue of racism. It can take years, however, for people to trust you enough to listen to your pain. When I first arrived at the congregation I now serve, I preached a sermon on driving while Black. I shared my experiences of being pulled over three times for being in wealthy White areas while visiting members and officiating at a wedding. Some members responded by saying I sounded so angry—as if I had no right to be angry. However, I didn't feel angry at the time. Nearly thirteen years later while preaching on Black Lives Matter, I expressed my anger, my sadness, and my frustration about the deaths of Black and Latinx men and women at the hands of the police and received a standing ovation. Of course this didn't stop one member from saying I was preaching to the choir.

I have always experienced the phrase *preaching to the choir* as a dismissal of what I am saying. It says we already know about, understand, embrace, and are tackling the issue, so why are you telling us? You should be out there telling others. It's hard to respond, "Well then, the choir needs a serious tune-up."

Much depends on how I raise the issues of race and racism and in what context they are lifted up. If I use humor and confession, it is much easier to disarm people and help them open up to their own experiences of excluding and being excluded. It is also much easier to lift up issues of race when I speak from my own experience, my own pain and frustration. If I say, "We all are part of the solution" and not "You are the problem," if it is something we need to work on together, people often feel less attacked than

I come from a testifying religious tradition, not a confessing tradition. I come from a tradition where you stand, in the midst of the people, and speak your pain out loud. We call the pain into the room, and everybody in the room is called to attend to it. That is what unity is. That is what church is. We are called to attend to each other the way that we really are, not our passing selves. "Church" is about building places where we can process pain and struggle as well as love and celebration. This is "Strength-in-the-Valley" theology. Unitarian Universalism has a "Mountaintop" theology. But you cannot really get to the mountaintop until you've been in the valley. You can't just skip over the struggle. As an institution, Unitarian Universalism does Easter without Good Friday. So Unitarian Universalism struggles with how we, as a religious body, can build a structure for learning how to hold pain, and I think that one way Unitarian Universalism tries to do that quickly is to cheat and "steal" it from other people's traditions. The harder and slower route is to be in relationship with communities of color. There are things I've learned in the African-American religious community, things I hear from people in the Hispanic Catholic tradition, things I hear from the Muslim traditions, from indigenous peoples of faith. This knowledge and experience can enrich Unitarian Universalism. When I am invited into Unitarian Universalism, when those from these other traditions are invited in, all that they have to offer must be invited in.

REV. NATALIE MAXWELL FENIMORE

if I tell them they need to look at themselves and what they are doing to contribute to the racism in the world. And yet working on racism is not why I became a minister. I personally find it exhausting and not very rewarding.

I used to say I didn't go into ministry to be the "Black minister." I want to simply be the minister, the best minister I can be. There are two self-deceptions in this. The first is that somehow I believed everyone could overlook my looks, my experiences, and my connection to Black history. The second is the idea that I can keep all the pain, anger, celebration, and joy of being Black locked up in a box.

Keeping in the suffering you experience from daily acts of racism is not healthy. I have stuffed so much that at times I feel I

———

I have experienced anxiety and depression, and I find a direct correlation to the work of being a UU minister of color. I don't talk about it very often. I take medication every day. I wonder how many of us have the same diagnosis. I wonder how common it is for UU religious professionals of color to suffer from anxiety and depression.

REV. MARISOL CABALLERO

Naming your story out loud can be a ministry to a lot of people; they will feel permission to do the work of dealing with anxiety and depression because you said that out loud, and I just think that's good ministry to say that out loud. It's permission-giving.

REV. LAUREN SMITH

I am off the charts ENFP, extroverted beyond the wall.
Since I've been in ministry, believe you me, I'm coming
so close to becoming an introvert. That's something that's
changed in me, inside. I am a totally extroverted ENFP,
but when I am in my UU settings, I have become
something quite different on the Myers–Briggs scale.

REV. DR. HOPE JOHNSON

Religious professionals of Color get sick more often.
That's just real. That's just something we all need to
think about. We need to take better care of ourselves
when we can, before we get the diagnosis it seems
that we will inevitably get.

REV. DR. HOPE JOHNSON

———

am going to burst. Finding allies who have been or can be trained to recognize the racial dynamics occurring at any given moment and to lift them up in noncombative ways, either at the moment or in private, is an effective way to address situations you feel unable to speak to at that time. I've seen allies do this, and it feels so good not to be the one who is the focus. And yet it is important to realize that having allies does not always translate into good outcomes. The minister of color may still be blamed for any discomfort or hurt that may arise.

I would argue that Black men aren't the only ones "seen as a threat in some form." As a Black woman, I have also had parishioners act afraid of me. In my fourth year of ministry with the church I now serve, a member of the congregation accused me of "battering her." I had gone to visit her with the Committee on

The thing about being intimidating is just really weird to me. At some point in the parish, I just threw up my hands, because I couldn't be anybody else. There was stuff I was just not going to tolerate, and I really didn't care if they were mad at me. When congregants say, "I'm just intimidated by you," I feel like saying, "See your therapist." What am I supposed to do about that? There's a part of us that hasn't learned yet to say, "That's your issue. Quit bringing me your issues. I'm not cleaning up behind you and all your shit." They want to bring it to you like you are the person who's supposed to take it out. It's true. They think I'm a magic Negro like Bagger Vance. A big part of our discernment is about whether this is race or people's issues about authority, and there's a moment when I don't really care which one it is, just stop bringing it to me. But you have to pick when you're actually going to say that. Just because you have a voice and an opinion, you're automatically intimidating, and it's ridiculous. I learned how not to let it have anything to do with me. It's complicated. There are just so many layers of stuff, things that people won't say to me because I went to Yale or because I worked with the New York Times. They couldn't ask if I wrote my own sermons because I'd written books by then, so it all became "You're scary."

REV. ROSEMARY BRAY MCNATT

Ministry because she was telling everyone, except me, that she was concerned about me. Although I had Committee on Ministry members present at the time who said I was kind and gracious, a number of members of the congregation believed I had battered an eighty-year-old woman. It took years to repair the damage to my ministry and even longer to repair the personal damage. Black men have called me intimidating, and I think some people, even people of color, take my introversion as arrogance. Black women are often perceived as loud and angry. These perceptions further complicate our ability to use our ministerial authority effectively.

I have been fortunate in my life to attend a couple of workshops on internalized oppression. I agree with Walter that it is important to look at the way the dehumanization and devaluing of people of color affects ministers of color in our attempts to live authentically. Stepping up and accepting the authority we have as ministers is easier when we are more comfortable with ourselves. However, no matter how much work a minister of color does uncovering internalized oppression, having colleagues with whom you can process your experiences is also helpful. Even when you know yourself and are comfortable with your position, racism can diminish your soul. Sharing such experiences with others who understand helps lift the burdens of loneliness and isolation so many of us feel. Colleagues of color can also help you distinguish issues of racism from issues of Unitarian Universalist anti-clergy sentiment and identify where the two might mingle.

An important piece of being prepared and maintaining a strong sense of self is having regular spiritual practice. Praying, chanting, meditating, journaling—whatever you can do to center yourself and stay balanced—is vital. When I make time to chant, I am able to release some pent-up pain and frustration. As I concentrate on the words and my breathing, I am lifted out of my current situation and transported to a place of joy.

An important learning for me was that stress is a lived emotion. It's physical, embodied in our being. A couple of years ago, I was navigating the stress of ministry and all the additional layers of personal and family life that we all have to navigate. It got to the point that I was getting physical symptoms. I was getting stomach cramps, and I actually thought there might be some serious GI problem with me. I went in and had a whole battery of tests done. Following an endoscopy, I was in the recovery room, coming out of sedation, and the GI doctor said, "You're basically fine. Yeah, sure a little bit of acid reflux, but you should go hit a punching bag." So I joined a boxing gym the next day. It was one of the best things I've ever done in my life! The amount of crap I get out of my system simply by hitting a punching bag is immense and it is good. Really good. I strongly recommend it. What I didn't fully connect with until I took those boxing classes was that I was embodying this energy and not finding a way to release it. We each have to find what works for us. Some people are able to release stress and negative energy through meditation. I'm not, so I need an embodied practice that involves physically getting it out, and what I needed to release included anger. I needed to get stress and anger out of my system, so boxing was perfect. As clergy, we aren't always thinking about our physical wellness. Doing the work of ministry, we lose sight of the physicality of ministry.

REV. MANISH MISHRA-MARZETTI

People of color are not prepared for so many things when we come into Unitarian Universalism and become religious leaders. Ministers of color need to be comfortable with the fact that we are not pied pipers of people of color. The congregation's disappointment over not becoming more diverse after they called a minister of color can be projected onto the minister. Instead of asking themselves what they might be doing to be more diverse, the congregation places blame on the minister of color. Second, there is a danger in holding racism too much in the forefront of our minds. We may miss opportunities to do transformative ministry if we constantly fight against every instance of racism we see. Sometimes we just have to let shit go.

It is a strange experience for many people of color—having a foot in many different doors and not yet fully embraced in any of them. We are all so different and yet the perception of others often dictates how successful we feel in our ministries. Striving to be fully integrated and embodied can be a lifelong struggle for many of us. It takes a lot of work and a lot of patience to not let the perception of others block the wonderful work of ministry we want to do.

CALL ME REVEREND SWEETIE
Rev. Cheryl M. Walker

WE ARE CALLED *Reverend*, we are called *ministers*, we are
called *pastors*, we are called *servant leaders*. These are traditional terms applied to clergy, especially those from traditionally
Christian religions. They have been used for centuries to describe
predominantly male clergy serving in congregations where the
racial makeup of the congregation is aligned with the racial
identity of the clergyperson. In that context, these words aptly
describe a relationship where the authority and power of the
clergyperson are rarely questioned and the roles of the clergyperson and laypeople are clearly defined. Regardless of the polity, it
is understood that the Reverend/minister/pastor/servant leader is

---

*When I was doing services in Spanish in San Jose,
the Latinxs who came from the Catholic Church
would say, "Where is the priest?" I said, "I am."
They said, "No, the one who preaches." They had
difficulty identifying preaching with a woman,
because in the Catholic Church there is no such
thing as a female priest. They would think I was a
nun. It was a difficult thing to explain. They asked
me, "Why don't you bring a man to the pulpit so
people would know there's authority here?"*

REV. LILIA CUERVO

the spiritual head of the congregation and, as such, is empowered and authorized to lead.

But what happens when the clergyperson is a woman? What happens when the racial identity of the clergyperson is not the same as that of the majority of the congregation? Do these terms for the religious leader still apply? If so, are they helpful or harmful? How does the language of ministry either foster or hinder the authority of the clergyperson?

As an African-American, lesbian woman, it is clear to me that each of these terms has a profound effect on my ministry and how I am perceived within and beyond the congregation where I serve. The terms have an effect on every minister, but the language of ministry has a particular impact on the power dynamics of ministers of color serving in predominantly White congregations.

What Shall I Be Called?

Recently, a newly ordained minister, Tom Bozeman, posed this question on the Unitarian Universalist Ministers Association Facebook page:

> I am a new minister (just ordained 10 days ago and starting my first actual job as a Rev. in August) and have a very simple question for you all:
> I've been asked how I would like people to refer to me. Would I prefer "Tom" or "Rev. Tom" or whatever else?
> I've never actually given this much thought and am curious about your thoughts on this.

The question generated much discussion. What should we be called as ordained Unitarian Universalist ministers? Does it matter? Should we use the title *Reverend*, or does it create a barrier for some people? Is it correct to use *Reverend Tom*, or should it be

Reverend Bozeman? As to be expected among any group of Unitarian Universalists, there was no agreement on what Tom should be called.

Missing from the discussion was any conversation about the authority and power inherent in the choice of what to be called. It was clear that our colleagues (almost all of them in this discussion were White) did not think the conversation was necessary because they thought their authority would be accepted without question. No one thought the title mattered much at all.

But titles do matter, and they matter especially for ministers of color and other clergy who have traditionally been at the margins in our congregations.

Depending upon our social location, either we are readily granted personal authority or we must earn it in our congregations. This fact was acknowledged at the very beginning of a 2013 report by the UUA Commission on Appraisal, *Who's in Charge Here?*

> The cultural standard of a white, straight, male minister is still in play though this describes a shrinking minority of actual Unitarian Universalist ministers. The extent to which a given minister varies from this standard impacts the way congregations and colleagues grant and withhold authority from that minister. This means that our struggles around authority and ministry fall most heavily on those furthest from the center of power and privilege in our national and Unitarian Universalist cultures.

Ministers of color should realize early on that their congregations will not automatically grant them personal authority as ministers. Therefore, it becomes important that the office of minister is the basis for the minister's authority in the beginning of their relationship with a congregation. One way to claim the authority of the office is by the title we choose to use.

In the congregation where I serve, I am known as Reverend Cheryl. Traditionally speaking, it should be Reverend Walker, but I chose not to use my last name for two reasons. First, it seemed too formal, too stiff. I may introduce myself as Reverend Walker in certain settings outside the congregation, but within the congregation I prefer the less formal Reverend Cheryl. It gives a sense that, while a professional boundary exists between congregants and me, the wall is not so high that we are more strangers than fellow travelers in the adventures of church life. The second reason I do not use Reverend Walker is that Walker is not my ancestral name; it was a name given to my ancestors by the people who owned them. It is a slave name, so I have no fondness for it.

From the beginning of my ministry with this congregation, I have insisted that people call me Reverend. One Sunday, a dear member of the congregation greeted me by calling me "Sweetie." I know she meant it as a term of endearment, and so I was not offended in the least. However, I informed her, "It's Reverend Sweetie to you, Dear." We both shared a laugh, but she understood why it was important she not call me Sweetie. Now she calls me Reverend Sweetie when she is especially cheerful, but she always calls me Reverend Cheryl when we are doing official church business. It's an inside joke. This was not the first time I've corrected someone who wanted to be inappropriately informal. I am also called Reverend Mama, Reverend Honey, Reverend Dear, and the RC by some. Everyone now knows that whatever they want to call me, a "Reverend" has to be before it, and I'm okay with that.

In the previous congregation I served, I didn't insist on being called Reverend Cheryl. It was not the custom in that congregation. Everyone was called by their first name. That was fine for the two senior ministers; no one questioned whether they were ministers in the congregation. But the custom had a different effect on me. On too many occasions to count, I would hear members talk about how grateful they were for the ministers, and they would name only the two White male ministers. I don't know if it would have made a difference if I had insisted on being called Reverend in that congregation, but I do know that although I never questioned whether my White male colleagues recognized my religious authority, they were seen as ministers by the members and often I was not.

My contention is that ministers of color should insist on being called Reverend for a variety of reasons. First, we have earned that title. It takes a fair amount of time, no small amount of money, and a long process of discernment to attain the title of Reverend

———

I now serve a congregation that, in recent decades, has been on a first-name basis with the White ministers who have served them, and so the question arises, why this formality? I haven't really known how best to talk about this, and my experience of religious leadership and authority is different for me, as an Asian American, than it is in the African-American tradition. In the Asian traditions, it's not so much formality as it is respect for the role of this person in your life. So we do not even think about calling a Hindu priest by their first name. We call them Pandit or Guru, and add the honorific Ji, which is the same as saying Sir or Madam. It's in the fiber of my being, in my culture, that this is how you relate to the role, with these signs of respect that the role matters to you, that who that person is and what they're doing in your life matters to you.

REV. MANISH MISHRA-MARZETTI

within Unitarian Universalism. We didn't just sign on to the Internet and pay twenty-five dollars; we went through an arduous process that made many of us question whether this was indeed the right faith for us. We are called to take as our own the history of a people who are not our own people. We are called to understand cultures that are not ours and learn to navigate well these cross-cultural differences. The path to ordination is harder for most of us than for our White colleagues, and it's hard enough for them. We should use the title because we have earned it.

Being called Reverend is also a way of insisting on respect as ministers who have a level of authority in our congregations. When I first arrived in Wilmington, North Carolina, I made some changes to the way worship was done. Primarily, I changed the order of things and did not bring back spoken joys and sorrows after the interim minister removed them from the liturgy. I received a slew of e-mails telling me to bring them back, to which I replied, "I will think about it." Then the question came: "Who are you to decide?" To which I replied, "I'm the minister. That's why I'm called Reverend Cheryl." That was enough of an answer for some, and for some it was not. Almost to a person, the ones for whom it was not enough were also the people who wanted to call me Cheryl and not Reverend Cheryl. The longer I have been the minister, the less I have to exert my authority, and the more authority is granted me. But in the beginning, respect for the title meant respect for the authority that comes with it.

A final reason ministers of color should insist on the title Reverend is to get people accustomed to using the term so that, when they are in the larger community, it is not something they have to think about. While it may be the custom in many UU congregations to call ministers by their first names, this is not true in all faith communities. Calling one's minister by their first name is seen by many outside the UU tradition as disrespectful.

For ministers of color to be called by our first names by White congregants is seen as especially disrespectful and undermines our authority in the larger community. Acclimating congregants to calling us Reverend helps them avoid situations where they would be seen as disrespecting us, and by extension, all clergy. And it helps us avoid the embarrassment of seeming to be disrespected.

———

A reporter from Reuters wanted to speak to me about our Black Lives Matter banner. She wanted to know if we'd just put it up. I told her we'd had it up for about two years. She said, "Where are all the clergy?" I started naming people. She was thinking of Al Sharpton and Jesse Jackson. She was looking for male clergy. She thinks the voice of the church is a Martin Luther King–type icon. There are plenty of people of color who don't sound like Martin Luther King or Jesse Jackson. You show up female, even in a chaplaincy setting, and you don't look like what they expect, White or wearing a collar, and they say, "Where's the priest?" It's cultural.

REV. DR. SUSAN NEWMAN MOORE

———

Ministers of color, by virtue of our divergence from the cultural standard of ministers as White, straight, and male, must use all the tools available to us to establish our authority in our congregations. One of the more important tools we have is the power of the office of minister, and we claim that power by claiming the title of Reverend.

Can I Speak to the Pastor?

Regional differences in language and culture also come into play. I am a native New Yorker. I was born in New York Hospital, in the county of New York, in the city of New York, in the state of New York. You can't be more of a New Yorker than I am. I now live in Wilmington, North Carolina, a different culture in many, many ways. I have had to use all my cultural competency skills to navigate the differences. From learning that when you order tea in a restaurant the default is iced and sweet to learning how to introduce myself and my role in the congregation. I learned all these things through the primary way we learn about most cultural differences: I did them wrong. I wanted hot tea and got iced tea; I introduced myself as the minister, and I should have said the pastor.

I first began to notice that I was introducing myself incorrectly when a White person came to the door of the church and I said hello and introduced myself as the minister, Reverend Cheryl. They asked if they could speak to the pastor. "I am the pastor," I replied. And with a look of surprise they said, "Okay, can I speak to you?" This was the first of many times I observed that when I said I was the *minister* there was a distinctly different reaction than when I said I was the *pastor*. The minister is someone who does something at a church; the pastor is the spiritual leader of a congregation. As a Unitarian Universalist, I was given the not so subtle message that ministers are never called pastors, because Unitarian Universalists are not sheep! Yet here I was in a place where being called a pastor was a sign of utmost respect. How to navigate the two cultures?

I am the only minister of color in Wilmington who leads a majority White congregation. For the most part, eleven A.M. on Sunday is still the most segregated hour, not just in Wilmington but across the country. Using the term *pastor* becomes even more

*I came into the parish from serving as president of the
UUA, so I came with huge credibility. My goal was not to
leave that experience of the UUA presidency behind me—
I learned a huge amount in that work—but to establish a
different way of being with the people in the congregation
that called me. I asked them what they would like to call
me. They said "Bill." I said, "Fine. You can also call me
Rev. Sinkford, Rev. Bill, or Pastor." "What does pastor
mean?" I did my riff about the cultural meaning of
that, so I did not have to work as hard to establish my
authority in the congregational setting and I could be
more flexible in terms of names. I think it's much
gendered. I'm also tall. All these play in.*

REV. DR. WILLIAM SINKFORD

––––––

important in such a position, especially when I am interacting with
pastors and members of predominantly Black congregations. I
always refer to myself as the pastor of the Unitarian Universalist
Congregation in Wilmington. When I do so, I am invited to the
clergy table as an equal. When I do not, I am somehow seen as
less than other clergy.

The problem with calling myself the pastor comes from within
my congregation. Many of them, especially those who have
migrated to North Carolina from Northern states, find it difficult to use the term *pastor* and are none too pleased that I use it.
Native Southerners have less of a problem with the term, though
sometimes they have admitted they have difficulty thinking of
a woman or a Black woman as a pastor, but they are willing to
work on it. This is not as true for Northerners, who often show

disdain for the Southern tradition and, by extension, the African-American tradition.

If UUs did not do any cross-cultural work with other churches or institutions, the inability of White congregants to refer to ministers of color as the pastors of congregations would not be a problem. But Unitarian Universalists say they want to interact and work with congregations of different cultures and, in particular, with African-American congregations on social justice issues. This puts me and other African-American ministers in a difficult position. If we allow our congregants to refer to us not as pastors but just as ministers, then we are embarrassed in front of other African-American people. We may be seen by African Americans as selling out our own culture to people who do not respect us enough to call us pastors. If we insist that UU congregants use language they are not comfortable with, they see us as not really Unitarian Universalist because we do not hold that tradition as superior. And we get stuck between a rock and a very hard place. We must choose which of our people we will align ourselves with.

We are hindered by the language of two conflicting cultures—one in which the term *pastor* is used to show respect and the

---

In my congregational setting, I would say that almost all the people of color call me Pastor, which I love, and it works for me. When they use that language in mixed company, I use it as a teaching moment to try to demystify some of it for European–American folks and make it okay to talk about some of this stuff.

REV. DR. WILLIAM SINKFORD

other in which it is met with derision. We become adept at crossing the cultural divide, but there comes a time when we cannot be the ones to cross that river alone. If the people in our congregations cannot cross the divide with us, then we must leave them behind, because in the end, we might not always be Unitarian Universalists, but we will always be people of color.

I May Serve Here, But I Am Not the Help

The term *pastor* versus *minister* is not the only language of ministry that can be a hindrance; in fact, I would contend that it is not even the most problematic; that would be the language of servitude. At a recent gathering of UU ministers, one attendee said that she wanted ministers to stop referring to congregations as "my" congregation and suggested we start saying "the congregation I serve." My reaction to what she said was swift and visceral. I could feel my body tense, and I had a hard time focusing on anything else that was said in her presentation. I was affronted by the idea of "serving" a congregation of mostly White people. Yet the language of servitude surrounds ministry. It is everywhere. In our faith tradition, in the absence of an agreed-upon theology, it is most often interpreted as serving the people in our congregations.

The language of ministry as servitude has its basis in Christian scriptures. In the Gospel of Mark, Jesus says to his disciples, "Whoever wants to become great among you must be your servant, and whoever wants to be first must be slave of all. For even the Son of Man did not come to be served, but to serve." From this passage and those similar to it, we have inherited the idea that ministers are to be servants. For people who are of a social location in which they are not servants, such as Jesus and his disciples, the idea of servitude is one of humility. It was a radical departure from the hierarchy of Rome. To this day, it is meant to remind ministers to embrace humility in the work. We are not above the people in our congregations but partners with them. We are here to work together and not to be their lords, as the Romans were lords to the people in Jesus's time.

However, for ministers of color, and especially for women ministers of color, *serving* the people in our congregations has very different meanings. While most of us do not have a personal history of being servants, we still carry with us the legacy of those who were forced by circumstance or by violence to be servants. The legacy is not just ours. American society has been built on the servitude of people of color. Carelessly using the language of servitude gives congregants permission to see ministers of color as servants. It undermines our authority as leaders in our congregations and in our faith tradition.

Ministers of color must be very careful in how we use the language of serving. We must be clear in our own minds first about what and/or whom we are serving. Are we serving God? Are we serving our highest purposes? Are we serving a greater mission for the church and society? Are we serving ourselves? We too must be wary of serving our own egos, and we too must show some humility before the awesomeness of existence. And we must be just as clear and articulate about whom we are *not* serving.

I am clear that first and foremost, I serve my God. I do that by serving God within the framework of Unitarian Universalism, at the Unitarian Universalist Congregation in Wilmington. I am equally clear that I do not serve the congregation or the people in it. I have been called by them to work for their greater good, not to work for them. To many White people in our congregations, it may seem like a matter of semantics, but it is not. Language matters, and how we use the language of serving matters greatly. Words are the primary tool of a minister; just as the words we use in worship, in conversations with congregants, and in meetings are important, so too are the words we use to describe ourselves as ministers. Ministers of color need to pay particular attention to how we are addressed and how we use the language of ministry. Used carelessly, language can cost us our authority and respect. Used carefully and positively, words can be the tools we wield to become true leaders in our congregations.

We are reverends. We are ministers. We are pastors. We are never servants.

RESPONSE TO CHERYL M. WALKER
Rev. Christina Shu

IN REFLECTING ON Cheryl's description of the connection between use of titles and pastoral authority, I was first drawn to her challenge of being specific about the language of service. I am deeply influenced by Rachel Naomi Remen's articulation in *Shambhala Sun* of the difference between fixing, helping, and serving. In her article "Helping, Fixing, or Serving," she says that words like *fixing* and *helping* invoke distance and hierarchy between people. However, she sees *serving* as representing an essential wholeness in relationships. She writes,

> We can only serve that to which we are profoundly connected. . . . When you help, you see life as weak. When you fix, you see life as broken. When you serve, you see life as whole. Fixing and helping may be the work of the ego, and service the work of the soul.

I see my role as providing service to my patients, meaning that we are profoundly connected, that we exist in a system of mutual interdependence, in which I, who am temporarily physically well, can be of support to someone who is temporarily sick. To introduce myself as a chaplain to another is to ask to companion to them on the journey of life and death, to engage in a process that is mutually enriching, restorative, and spiritually healing.

As a community minister and chaplain, I relate to the language of ministry as service in a different way than Cheryl does. I too recoil from the language of *servant minister* as I associate it with a history of Asian women being forced into lives of servitude, and a history of stereotyping Asian Pacific Islander women as servile, submissive, and voiceless. However, in my position I do not serve a majority-White UU congregation as a minister. I am a health-care chaplain and serve a dynamic, ever-changing population of patients, families, and staff who reflect the greater city of Los Angeles. Serving the spiritual relationships in my community is different than being a servant. I use the language of *serving* to imply shared companionship, mutuality, interdependence, and spiritual wholeness, which is integral to the role of being a chaplain.

To serve wholeness in other people, I must begin with an understanding of myself as a whole person. This is part of the formation process of clinical pastoral education as well as ministry formation, a process to develop my understanding of identity, theology, personality, important relationships, and being in the world. A significant part of my identity is my Chinese-American heritage and family history, growing up Unitarian Universalist in Southern California, and belonging to a family that valued justice and civil rights and celebrated Lunar New Year. Understanding my own identity, including my ethnic identity, and honoring my strengths and vulnerable edges is part of providing wholehearted, authentic presence with others. My pastoral authority really comes from knowing myself, loving myself, and believing in myself. I draw on my beliefs in interdependence and interconnection, on the importance of relationships and shared decision making, on the use of silence and creative rituals—these are skillful uses of who I am in pastoral care.

With this grounding, I can be flexible in my theological language and in how I approach families of different cultures and backgrounds. At times I choose to be silent, choose to speak out, choose to pray or not to pray, choose to conform to my patient's assumptions about a chaplain, and choose to defy those assumptions. I know that connecting to another person of color and

*Community ministers often don't have all of the
resources that parish ministers have. We don't often use
good officers in the same way. Where can we find that
support? Most of my parish work is now pulpit supply,
so I don't have the relationships with the congregation
when issues come up, and I don't know how to respond,
because I'm not going to be there next week. I'm not
going to be there in five minutes because then I'm going
home, and there's no place to deal. That's why I need
a minister, so I can just talk about what happened.*

REV. DARRICK JACKSON

———

reflecting their experience of oppression, connecting to an Asian American over shared love of food or respect for elders, and connecting with a nonreligious person over humanism are all ways of drawing from my identity and using it skillfully to create a bond with another person. I seek to be both a young, female Chinese-American chaplain and *your* chaplain, not in spite of who I am but because of who I am.

Grounding myself in my own whole, authentic presence, I am able to go out and serve wholeness in others. Sometimes others are challenged at first to accept this presence and authority in me, and in these cases, the use of titles—Reverend, Pastor, Chaplain—can help. I am aware that whoever I meet may have wildly varying assumptions and relationships to these titles or may have no understanding at all about the role of a health-care chaplain.

I regularly introduce myself to strangers of all different backgrounds with the words "Hi, I'm Christina, and I'm one of the chaplains here to support you." Many of the people I meet have a television-derived image of what a chaplain should look like—elderly, White, male, wearing a priest's collar. They believe a chaplain visits only to provide Last Rites. When I show up, many are shocked to find out a chaplain could look like me. They are also shocked to find that the chaplain can support them at different stages of illness, that the chaplain can support them even if they have stopped attending religious services or are atheist or Pagan, that the chaplain wants to support them just as they are. I must constantly explain that I'm not here to proselytize, judge, or condemn but to listen, to reflect, and to facilitate spiritual meaning and growth. These are also times when skillful use of my pastoral authority and competence—deep listening and empathy—opens up the relationship into seeing one another as whole.

On one occasion, after I entered a patient's room and introduced myself as a chaplain, the patient's family member started up with an unusual line of questioning: "Are you Chinese? Are

---

I'm thinking about the idea of serving and surrender in ministry. In pastoral care, while I have to know myself to know what's mine and not, I also have to set that aside in some ways to be present. In other areas of ministry, I have to center myself in ways that are actually uncomfortable and take a very different kind of authority. That kind of relationship is complicated because, as people of color, we often go through a whole re-centering liberation thing to claim ourselves. I find a dramatic tension between the re-centering for the sake of claiming oneself and the ministry of care.

REV. MITRA RAHNEMA

you familiar with *qi gong*? Have you seen it be effective on patients?" *Qi gong* is a form of ancient Chinese medicine. I said kindly and firmly that I was not familiar with *qi gong*, nor could I offer any advice on its efficacy. After this exchange, the family member lost interest and ended the conversation. I *wish* I had said, "I hear that you really care about your loved one, and that you're worried that our medical treatment isn't working. What has this experience been like for you?" That would have been a way of transforming an interaction in which someone saw me only for my Asian-American identity into a way of serving wholeness for this family member.

Patients and their families often make assumptions and judgments or question my ability to be a chaplain. I also hear statements like "You're too young to be a chaplain!" or "What *kind* of

---

Decentering myself in response to microaggressions does take a toll, but I think that exercise of being a chaplain, of meeting so many different people throughout the day, means I could have one time in the morning when someone makes a racialized comment or says, "You seem too young," but then a visit right after that with someone who immediately gets what I'm there to do. When I'm able to let go of my initial, defensive response response and to use my pastoral authority as a chaplain, often my relationships with patients end up as very rich and fulfilling, and I feel I have served wholeness in that person and maybe changed their ideas about what a chaplain who looks like me can do.

REV. CHRISTINA SHU

chaplain are you?" and the recurring "What do you believe about Jesus Christ?" At times, microaggressions and questioning of my authority are exhausting. They can be frustrating barriers to offering spiritual care. However, much more often they are windows into new relationships, and that is energizing.

The role of a chaplain provokes respect, trust, and intimacy. I've had the privilege of a patient exclaiming as soon as I walk through the door, "Chaplain, you're just the person; I really need to talk to you." I have also had the privilege of other members of the health-care team stopping at the door when they see me with a patient and saying, "Oh, I'll come back later, your conversation is more important right now." The privilege of being asked to pray out loud for someone I met five minutes before is still humbling and transforming to me even after many years of practice.

A large urban hospital in Los Angeles is a fantastic place to work as a minister of color and a Unitarian Universalist. More than 50 percent of my patients are people of color of many faiths. I have the privilege of working alongside a staff of great cultural, ethnic, racial, and religious diversity; this benefits my understanding of my own identity and my UU theology. With my appearance, I've had a lot of opportunity for people to assume that I'm a nurse, a physician, a volunteer, and a patient's family member, and I meet people in all those positions every day who look like me. The racial diversity in health-care staffing emboldens me. I feel empowered when I sit at patient-plan-of-care rounds and look around the table and see an interdisciplinary staff primarily made up of people of color.

Every day I try to exercise multicultural and multireligious theological flexibility. By this I mean that I'm constantly in the act of being present and developing empathy, intimacy, and spiritual connection with those who are different from me in racial, ethnic, cultural, religious, and gender identities and in countless other factors. The exercise of developing mutual and interdependent relationships with a diverse set of people, often in the setting of tragedy and crisis, *and* being able to let go of these relationships when a person leaves the hospital is akin to strengthening a muscle. To listen, to carry emotional burdens, and to share in sacred space and time with different sets of people throughout one's day requires practice and continual stretching and repetition. It can be tiring, and yet it is rewarding. The experience has given me a deepening insight into the lives of my neighbors in my city, their faith, sorrows, grief, hopes, and joys—insight into otherwise hidden inner dimensions of people I might otherwise not meet. In strengthening this multicultural muscle, I find my own faith challenged and expanded in a way that calls me into ever-deeper ways of serving as a minister.

Finally, as a chaplain, I am part of the hospital institution and at the same time an outsider, a spiritual representative in the world of medicine. People of color can hold a reasonable distrust of medical institutions, which have often failed to provide equitable health care to all. A chaplain can act as a bridge, a fellow and trustworthy "outsider" in the hospital. One role of a chaplain can be cultural broker—someone who can interpret and create understanding between a patient's cultural, racial, or religious worldview and the perspective of the medical team. Chaplains are also cultural advocates, standing beside patients and advocating respect, accommodation, or inclusion. Chaplains are often looked to as representatives of diversity, as we recognize that different peoples and cultures have very different ways of seeing illness, hospitalization, death, and healing. As a community institution, the hospital needs chaplains not only to preserve the soul and spirituality of the tradition of healing but also to serve the needs of an increasingly diverse and multicultural world.

Long before I came to recognize my vocation and identity as a minister, I already knew myself to be called as a chaplain. As a chaplain who is also a woman of color and a Unitarian

Universalist, I ground myself in an understanding of who I am and my own authority and power in order to provide spiritual care to whoever walks through the hospital door. My model for chaplaincy is one of spiritual companionship, of creating a relationship of trust with another person so that I can accompany them on their own spiritual journey. I seek to symbolize power with rather than power over and to demonstrate this in my relationships with my patients. It is from a profound feeling of humility and respect for the wholeness present in every person that I claim my identity as a chaplain.

Discussion Cues
Rev. Mitra Rahnema

M ANY THEMES EMERGED from our essays, responses, and discussion. Therefore we fleshed out some of those themes and offered questions for your reflection. We encourage you to pick the questions that resonate with and challenge you just enough to delve deeper into your story and your experience of the book, and help you make connections. The ultimate goal is to increase our collective capacity for love and to care for those who are centering into the future of Unitarian Universalism.

Identity vs. Role

Much of the preparation for professional religious leadership, and the practice of our Unitarian Universalist faith, is a process of finding our authentic voice and then discerning how we want to use our unique voice to help the larger world. It is a process of liberation, but the actual practice of ministry, in which we are trying to help others connect with their authentic selves and deepen their spiritual lives, can be especially complicated for people of color in predominantly White communities. Sometimes it means finding ourselves at a distance from our own authenticity and our need to bear witness to the racial undercurrents in our society.

- Think of a time when you set your racial identity aside in order to meet someone "where they are." How did you discern what to do in that situation? How did it turn out for you and how do you feel about your choice in hindsight?

Would you make the same choice again knowing what you know now?

- We all have to make choices about when to speak up, to interrupt, to say, "That hurt" or "Can we think about that another way?" and when not to. Do you think the expectations of "right relationship" are different for religious professionals of color? Can you articulate the values and priorities that help you with that decision making in the moment? What happens to your sense of self and sense of ministry?
- What particular issues in your community and in our larger culture reveal a conflict between your need for authenticity and attending to the needs of others as a religious leader?
- Our writers express a longing for a Unitarian Universalist community that can meet our lives where we are, that believes our stories just as they are, that will talk about the struggle and evils in addition to the "progress." Do you resonate with these longings? Where do you turn to search for what you need in spiritual community? Do you have a community that welcomes your whole self?

Pastoral Role vs. Prophetic Role

Our writers talk about the choices we make between the pastoral and prophetic roles of ministry. We are all steeped in these two roles of ministry as essential parts of our work. One can be exemplified by the archetype of Moses on the mountaintop receiving God's word, gaining strength and inspiration, looking toward a new promise for the people. This is the role of the prophet, the leader who helps us to imagine, points the way forward, inspires us to help one another, and bends that arc of justice. It requires audacity and a vision bigger than anything in front of us. A second archetype is that of a pastoral Jesus washing the feet of his disciples. This is the role of the servant, that of humbling oneself and caring for one another. It is about love and tenderness—lifting up another so they know and can experience their own worth. We know Moses and Jesus both held many facets to their ministries, and we know that the pastoral and prophetic are really interdependent acts. The archetypes of Moses as prophet and Jesus as servant are models and necessary for any healthy ministry, but both also present complications for religious leaders of color.

- Which role, the prophetic or pastoral, comes more naturally to you in your UU community? Why do you think that is?
- Which role does your community tend to expect you to prioritize? Do those expectations impact your racial identity?
- What are the racial implications of the prophet? Does your community accord you the authority to fulfill the prophetic role? Does their understanding of that role mesh with yours? Are there particular issues that you feel more or less free to be prophetic about? Why? Are there issues your community expects you to be more involved in or actions they expect you to take because of your racial identity? As a person of color, do you struggle with decisions about whether to take certain positions or actions, such as risking arrest, in particular ways that are unrecognized by your community?
- The pastoral role is often articulated as a "servant" role. How does that language resonate for you as a person of color in culturally White communities? Are you sometimes forced to choose between pastoral care and self-care? For instance, have you been asked to give spiritual guidance to someone struggling with racist thoughts? How do you tend to respond? And what has been the cost for you? Where do you turn for pastoral care for yourself?
- If the prophetic role and the pastoral role are both essential to ministry, how do you balance them? When have you had

to choose between them? Would you make the same choice again if given the chance?

Commitment to Unitarian Universalism

Our writers express profound commitment to Unitarian Universalism, both its tradition and its promise. As Manish Mishra-Marzetti said, "Unitarian Universalism is who I am and it's in my bones." This book offers story after story of religious leaders of color contending with the faith that we chose to center in our lives—theologies that offer sacred attention to multiple truths, expanding consciousness, centering the margins, and revealing unseen beauty. We also have had to look at what it is now and "let it go" as Manish says. For many of us, while Unitarian Universalism resonates deeply, commitment to it can cause painful dissonance because it often requires moving away from a community that affirms our racial identity. But we have been called to this faith and religious leaders of color are acutely aware of that call that is bigger than any of us. Many of us are not going anywhere.

- Have you experienced dissonance between Unitarian Universalism's promise and its current reality?
- Have you ever been tempted to leave Unitarian Universalism as your primary faith home? Why? If you stayed, what keeps you here?
- Is there a spiritual community or tradition that you miss? What do you most miss about it? Where do you turn now to find what you're missing? Can you imagine Unitarian Universalism filling that need now or in the future?
- Have you ever considered resigning your position as a religious leader in Unitarian Universalism? Why? What have you considered doing instead? If you decided to stay in your position, what motivated that decision?

- Have you ever considered taking a larger leadership role in the faith? How has your identity as a person of color affected your decision?
- Some of our writers expressed a love for and commitment to the "Unitarian Universalism that is not yet." What does that future Unitarian Universalism look like to you?
- What special gifts do you think that people of color, and particularly religious leaders of color, bring to Unitarian Universalism? What special gifts do you bring? Are they seen and recognized?
- If you are struggling with questions about whether to stay with your UU community, your position as a religious leader, or Unitarian Universalism itself, what would help you want to stay? What would help you thrive and grow spiritually in your chosen community and in your ministry?

Be the Change

Many of us resonate with the powerful words of Mahatma Ghandi: "Be the change you wish to see in the world." When there is pain we wish to bring comfort. When there is injustice we wish to bring just witness. We are told to, as Reinhold Niebuhr wrote, "comfort the afflicted and afflict the comfortable." These words point toward a savvy ministry that powerfully responds to suffering and disruption. Yet for religious professionals of color, it gets so much more complicated. Sometimes we are directly and indirectly "asked to be change agents," as Bill Sinkford remarks, a sort of "racial/cultural savior." At other times we are seen as the problem or disruption; people feel dis-comforted by our racial or cultural identities. Both projections can leave the religious leader out on their own, separated from the community they serve. While we want to be aligned with the vision of the collective, we become the "other."

- Have you been cast as a "change agent" for a church community? How did that play out? How did that feel? How did that influence your ministry?
- Have you ever felt your existence was a disruption? How did you respond? What were the consequences to your ministry and/or to your racial identity?
- What kind of stress does being seen as a change agent, cultural savior, or disruption put on you? What is the effect on your ministry, agency, and sense of call?
- Do you intentionally embrace or reject any of these roles? Do they empower or hinder your ministry? How?
- Do you ever feel that your work is "behind the scenes" and not recognized as an agent of change when you want it to be? What effect, if any, has this had on your ministry?

Other Themes

Our conversations in the conference that led to this book were so rich that they revealed many themes worth delving into. Here are some others that we want to particularly lift up:

- What is the effect on our careers when our colleagues and institutions expect us to lead primarily from our identity as people of color and not from the wholeness of our being? For instance, people of color may be expected to be leaders in anti-racism work when they feel more called to another kind of ministry, or expected to serve in congregations that have historically been focused on racial justice work or been led by people of color. Do we have the same agency as our White colleagues in choosing our work and following our calling?
- How are religious leaders of color asked to "pass"? How are we expected to repress our authentic selves? How does this expectation affect our careers and our ministries? Do you

have room to grow your relationship with your racial identity? How do we navigate the intersections between the primarily White UU communities in which we serve and our communities of color while being true to ourselves?

- How is your relationship with your colleagues throughout our denomination? Have you found solidarity? Have you found colleagues who can "get it"? Have you found colleagues suspicious of your abilities because of your race? What toll does that take on your ministry, your soul, and your loved ones?

What Helps?

At the end of our conference, we shared with each other our learnings from being in dialogue with one another. The following questions for reflection and discussion are based on that deep conversation about where we find hope, support, strength, and resilience.

- It's important for religious leaders of color to hold to one another in loving, humane, and compassionate ways. How have you experienced this personally? How can we offer this kind of solidarity to each other?
- Self-care is essential. How can we better care for our spiritual, physical, and emotional lives individually and collectively?
- People with different racial identities experience racism in very different ways. How can we share our stories and struggles with each other, under the umbrella of "people of color," in ways that honor our own truths and forge solidarity?
- Our identity as "the other" comes with strength as well as struggle. In what ways can we claim that identity and use it for good? What particular gifts and insights do we bring to our communities and to Unitarian Universalism because we are outsiders in positions of authority? How do our

experiences and stories broaden and deepen the experience of Unitarian Universalism for all?

- We need to value all forms of religious leadership as vital to making the Unitarian Universalism we want to see. Religious education, music leadership, membership coordination, and volunteer service are ministries that need to be lifted up, celebrated, and resourced along with ordained ministry. If you are a non-ordained religious leader of color, how have you contributed to your community and to the evolution of Unitarian Universalism from that particular location? Have you been able to make a difference in ways that a White colleague or an ordained minister could not? What stories can you share about the importance of non-ordained religious leaders of color? Do you feel your ministry is recognized, valued, and supported by other religious professionals?

- We need to center people of color more in UU antiracist, anti-oppressive, multicultural work. Too often UUs conduct this work with a focus on White experience and what White people need to do. How can we center yourselves in conversations around these issues so that our experience is recognized and our needs addressed? Do we know more about White Unitarian Universalism than White Unitarian Universalists know about us? How can we change that?

We hope you have found these texts and questions meaningful. We encourage the communities of color to make connections, listen deeply to each other, and love.

Some of the places that Unitarian Universalist people of color currently find community are:

Diverse and Revolutionary Unitarian Universalist
Multicultural Communities (DRUUMM):
druumm.onefireplace.org

Latino(a) Unitarian Universalist Network (LUUNA): luuna.org

Black Lives of Unitarian Universalism (BLUU): blacklivesuu.com

Annual multicultural retreat for religious professionals, "Finding Our Way Home": uua.org/multiculturalism/retreat

There are various other people of color—centered spaces emerging all the time. We encourage you to seek and connect.

If you would like to share your thoughts and/or find out about new opportunities to engage with this text that are currently being developed, please email centering@uuma.org .

About the Contributors

Rev. Summer Albayati serves as minister at the Unitarian Universalist Fellowship of Kern County in Bakersfield, California, and is a member of the Unitarian Universalist Ministers Association's Committee on Antiracism, Anti-Oppression, and Multiculturalism. She is the daughter of the late and legendary Iraqi musician Saadoun Al-Bayati, and has played the Sufi Islamic rhythms of his homeland in professional concerts with him since she was twelve years old.

Rev. Sofia Betancourt serves as assistant professor of Unitarian Universalist theologies and ethics at Starr King School for the Ministry and is a Ph.D. candidate at Yale University in the Department of Religious Ethics and African American Studies. Her work focuses on environmental ethics of liberation in a womanist and Latina feminist frame. She served for four years as the director of racial and ethnic concerns of the Unitarian Universalist Association, and her ministry centers on work that is empowering and counter-oppressive. Betancourt holds a B.S. from Cornell University with a concentration in ethnobotany, an M.A. and M.Phil. from Yale University in religious ethics and African American studies, and an M.Div. from Starr King. From April to June of 2017, she served as interim co-president for the Commission for Institutional Change for the UUA.

Rev. Dr. Orlanda Brugnola (1946–2016) served as a community, interim, and assistant minister during her almost forty years in ministry. She was a teacher, artist, organizer, chaplain, therapist, and mediator, among many other things. She taught philosophy, world religions, conflict resolution, and ministerial formation at a variety of universities and Seminaries. Rev. Brugnola was dedicated to interfaith dialogue, cultivating peace, and dismantling all forms of oppression throughout our world. She died during the writing of this book and her unfinished writing was not able to be published at this time. We are grateful for her participation in the creation of this book, for her wisdom and support. She is deeply missed.

REV. MARISOL CABALLERO is a Tejana from Austin, lifelong Unitarian Universalist, and a graduate of Union Theological Seminary. She currently serves the Unitarian Universalist Association's Faith Development Office as Faith Innovation Specialist. Within UU circles, Marisol serves on the Diverse and Revolutionary UU Multicultural Ministries (DRUUMM) Executive Committee, most recently co-creating and organizing the Global Majorities Collective, a project that intends to create a distinct UU people of color religio-cultural expression. She has also co-founded the Central Texas UUs of Color group that meets monthly and co-facilitates a small group people of color ministry in connection with The Church of the Larger Fellowship. Within her local community, Marisol is also a co-founder of W.M.E.N. (Women Ministers' Empowerment Network), an organization of progressive clergywomen of color in Central Texas; serves on the Board of Just Texas, an interfaith reproductive justice advocacy group; and is an active member of the Austin Justice Coalition.

REV. LILIA CUERVO is the first Latin American woman ordained as a Unitarian Universalist minister and the first full-time parish minister to offer the complete range of ministerial services in Spanish. She was the first woman to be installed as a parish minister at First Parish in Cambridge, Massachusetts. She is a co-founder of the Latina/o UU Networking Association (LUUNA), and the initiator of the Spanish-language Unitarian Universalist hymnal *Las voces del camino*. Prior to ministry, she was a demographer working in Colombia, Brazil, and the United States.

Rev. Natalie Maxwell Fenimore is part of the ministerial team at The Unitarian Universalist Congregation at Shelter Rock in Manhasset, New York. She is the minister of lifespan religious education. Rev. Fenimore has been director of religious education, parish minister, and minister of religious education in Unitarian Universalist congregations in Maryland, Virginia, and New York since 1998. She is a UUA-credentialed religious educator at the master's level and past president of the Liberal Religious Educators Association.

Rev. Dr. Kristen Harper has been the minister of the Unitarian Church of Barnstable, Massachusetts, for fifteen years. Prior to coming to Barnstable, she served communities in Lansing, Michigan, and Ormond Beach, Florida. She received her doctorate from Meadville Lombard Theological School in 1999. She has worked with HIV-positive women, men, and teenagers; with the Council on Aging; with teen mothers, youth leaders, and LGBT youth and young adults; and with interfaith organizations and sits on the Board of the Cape Cod Council of Churches.

Aisha Hauser, MSW, was born in Alexandria, Egypt, and her family moved to the United States when she was a toddler. Consequently, she didn't learn English until just before kindergarten. She started her professional career in the field of social work after earning an MSW from Hunter College in New York City. While working as the director of religious education for The First Unitarian Universalist Church of Essex County in Orange,

New Jersey, she was elected as secretary of the Board of Trustees of the Liberal Religious Educators Association. She later accepted the additional job of urban community ministry coordinator at First UU Church. Her dual role in the congregation afforded the opportunity to combine social justice work with religious education. She has completed the Religious Education Credentialing Program at the Associate Level and has been active with the UU community of ministers and religious educators of color, attending the yearly retreat called Finding Our Way Home. She has also worked for the Unitarian Universalist Association as children and families program director.

Rev. Darrick Jackson is the director of contextual ministry at Meadville Lombard Theological School. He is involved denominationally as treasurer of DRUUMM (the UU ministry for people of color) and as co-chair of both the UU Ministers Association CENTER Committee and the Institute for Ministerial Excellence. He is also the treasurer and workshop leader for Healing Moments (a ministry for people with Alzheimer's disease and their caregivers).

Rev. Dr. Hope Johnson serves as a congregational consultant for the Central East Region as well as minister of the Unitarian Universalist Congregation of Central Nassau in Garden City, Long Island, New York. She is also president of the Living Legacy Project, an organization that lifts up the lessons and legacy of the Civil Rights Movement. She has served as chair of the UUA Nominating Committee and the UUA Appointments Committee, as well as trustee of the UUMA Board, holding the portfolios of Anti-racism/Anti-oppression/Multiculturalism and Good Offices. She currently serves as trustee on the Unitarian Universalist Service Committee Board. She was a co-recipient of the President's Annual Award for Volunteer Service to the UUA.

Rev. Walter LeFlore is the settled minister at the Unitarian Universalist Fellowship of Poughkeepsie, New York. He is a graduate of Andover Newton Theological School. He serves on the UUMA Board of Trustees and co-chairs the Committee on Antiracism, Anti-oppression, and Multiculturalism. He is vice president of the Dutchess County Interfaith Council. For twenty years prior to ministry, he was principal of Organizational Systems Associates, providing management consulting primarily to Fortune 100 corporations.

Rev. Rosemary Bray McNatt, the president of Starr King School for the Ministry in Berkeley, California, previously served for thirteen years as senior minister of the Fourth Universalist Society in the City of New York. She is a graduate of Yale University and Drew Theological Seminary. She also worked as an editor and widely anthologized writer for more than twenty years before answering the call to ordained ministry. Her years of service to the UUA have included work on a number of committees, including the Committee on Urban Concerns and Ministry, the Task Force for Strategic Options for Beacon Press, the UUA Panel on Theological Education, and the UUA Board of Trustees. Her social justice work most recently included service as the convenor of OccupyFaithNYC, a multi-faith economic justice organization founded in the spirit of Occupy Wall Street, and a co-convenor of Moral Monday NYC, a multi-faith social justice group ispired by Rev. Dr. William Barber. In 2002, she helped to found the Unitarian Universalist Trauma Response Ministry.

Rev. Manish Mishra-Marzetti serves as senior minister of The First Parish in Lincoln, Massachusetts, a dual Unitarian Universalist Association and United Church of Christ member congregation. He has served extensively in Unitarian Universalist leadership, including as president of DRUUMM (our UU people of color organization); commissioner on the UUA Commission on Appraisal, co-authoring its report *Engaging Our Theological Diversity*; secretary of the Board of Starr King School for the Ministry; and an author and advocate of our 2007 General Assembly resolution confronting gender identity–related discrimination. He brings to the ministry his experience serving as a U.S. diplomat during the Clinton administration.

Rev. Dr. Susan Newman Moore was ordained by the United Church of Christ in 1983, becoming the seventh Black woman ordained in the denomination. She is currently the associate minister for congregational life and pastoral care at All Souls Church, Unitarian, in Washington D.C. In Atlanta, she was senior minister of First Congregational Church, UCC; chair of the Mayor's Commission on Community Relations; a member of the Governor's Blue Ribbon Panel on Welfare Reform; and executive director of Georgians for Children. She is an inductee into the Board of Preachers of the Martin Luther King Jr. Chapel at Morehouse College, which honors clergy for their lifetime work in social justice. She has also served as the religious coordinator for the Children's Defense Fund, director of public policy at the Religious Coalition for Reproductive Choice, and senior advisor for religious affairs to the mayor of the District of Columbia. She has been hailed by *Ebony Magazine* as one of the Top Black Women Preachers in America. As adjunct professor at the United Theological Seminary in Dayton, Ohio, she co-mentored the Wheeler-Newman Fellows, a doctorate of ministry degree program.

Rev. Peter Morales was elected president of the Unitarian Universalist Assocation in 2009. Previously, he served as the senior minister at Jefferson Unitarian Church in Golden, Colorado. He has also served as the director for district services at the UUA and sat on the UUA Board of Trustees, the Mountain Desert District Board, and the Executive Committee of the UUA.

Rev. Mitra Rahnema is a biracial Iranian-American lifelong Unitarian Universalist. She is currently offering her ministry at the Unitarian Universalist Church of Long Beach, California. Prior to Long Beach she served communities in Grosse Point, Michigan; Mission Viejo, California; and Kansas City, Kansas. She is currently a member of the UUMA Committee on Antiracism, Anti-Oppression, and Multiculturalism.

Rev. Adam Robersmith is an ordained Unitarian Universalist minister and spiritual director of multiracial heritage. He serves Second Unitarian Church in Chicago and has recently completed a Doctor of Ministry degree studying spiritual formation for Unitarian Universalists, particularly seminarians and ministers.

Rev. Christina Shu is the lead interfaith chaplain at Cedars-Sinai Medical Center in Los Angeles, California. She is also an affiliated community minister at Neighborhood Unitarian Universalist Church in Pasadena, California. She identifies as a Chinese-American woman.

Rev. Dr. William Sinkford currently serves as senior minister of First Unitarian in Portland, Oregon. From 2001 to 2009, he served as president of the Unitarian Universalist Association. A Unitarian Universalist since the age of fourteen, he was a youth leader in Unitarian Universalism in the 1960s but stepped away from our faith in the aftermath of what is commonly called the Black Empowerment Controversy. Returning to our faith after a decade "in the wilderness," he was called to the ministry and service on the staff of the Association before his election to the UUA presidency. He identifies as African American and was the first African American to lead a predominantly White denomination. From April to June of 2017 he served as interim co-president of the UUA.

Rev. Lauren Smith currently serves as co-minister at South Church in Portsmouth, New Hampshire, along with her husband, Rev. Chris Holton Jablonski. Her ties to Unitarian Universalism stretch back five generations. Her great-great-grandfather William Hazel was born a free black person in North Carolina. His family fled to the North a few years before the start of the Civil War. When he grew to manhood, William became a member of the First Parish in Cambridge.

Rev. Leslie Takahashi has been active in the Unitarian Universalist Association's conversation about race since she joined as a multiracial young adult. She is a co-author of *The Arc of the Universe Is Long: Unitarian Universalists, Anti-racism and the Journey from Calgary*. Her current passion is the day-to-day work of building beloved community at the Mt. Diablo Unitarian Universalist Church, where she serves as lead minister.

Rev. Cheryl M. Walker has served as the pastor of the Unitarian Universalist Congregation of Wilmington, North Carolina, since 2009. Prior to Wilmington, she served for four years as the assistant minister at the Unitarian Church of All Souls in New York City. She currently serves as the president of the Unitarian Universalist Ministers Association. She holds a bachelor's degree in mathematics from Springfield College and a master of divinity degree from Union Theological Seminary in the City of New York.